English China

PATTERNS & PIECES

Identification & Values

MARY FRANK GASTON

COLLECTOR BOOKS

A Division of Schroeder Publishing Co., Inc.

Front cover: Cream soup cup and saucer, a
floral pattern by Johnson Bros., circa 1913.
$75.00 – 95.00.
Back cover: Plate, Landscape pattern
by W. R. Midwinter, circa 1910.
$100.00 – 125.00.

Cover design by Beth Summers
Book design by Marty Turner
Cover photography by Charles R. Lynch

COLLECTOR BOOKS
P.O. Box 3009
Paducah, Kentucky 42002-3009

www.collectorbooks.com

Searching for a Publisher?

We are always looking for people knowledgeable within their fields. If
you feel that there is a real need for a book on your collectible subject
and have a large comprehensive collection, contact Collector Books.

Proudly printed and bound in the
United States of America

Contents

Dedication

To the girls of our family:
Melissa, Reagan, and Jordan

Acknowledgments

For *English China, Patterns and Pieces,* I would like to thank the following contributors:

A & B Auctions, Inc.	Becky Delik	Gregory Lewis	Anne Pratt Slatin
Gerald Abell	Julie Dolan	Patricia Lewis	Nel Slaughter
John Adams	Paula Drury	James B. McClenahan, M. D.	Gwen Steapp
Tom Ammann	Brenda Fancett	McKinney Avenue	Sara Stickler and J. B. Queen
Banowetz Antiques	Becky Frederico	Antiques Market	Gloria Swanson Antiques
Virl & Kathy Banowetz	Eiko Glade	Mr. and Mrs. John L. Melling	Stephanie Systema
Frantzen Photography	Judy Grant	Amy L. Miller	Jane Thomasson
Norma Barkdull	Debby Hagara	Thomas Nash	Jan and Dave Truax
James Beeman	Hazel Harp	Janet Nussberg-Makos	Veronica Tunler
Brenda L. Bentley	Audrey M. Harris	Andrew J. Pye	Margaret Vanlier
Daryl P. Black	Ruby Holland	Mary Ann Rapposelli	Kandy Waas
Lola Bradley	Susan Hoopes	Connie Reder	Doris Walker
Susan Bragg	Jo Ann Jones	Linda Richard	Susan E. Wallace
Debbie Cairns-LaRue	Mr. and Mrs. John Keck	Mike Richards	John White
Brenda B. Carlisle	Cheryl Koby	Claudette Saylor	Robert Yerby
Lisa Caryl	Alan Kushner	Janet L. Schryver	Sarah M. Zafra
Edith Clanton	Roy T. Leitza	Louise Singletary	

A number of examples from several of my other publications have been included in this book because they represented pieces or patterns of English china which were of interest. Therefore, I would also like to thank those many contributors, who, although they are not listed individually here, have indeed contributed to this new edition through their help with my earlier works: *Art Deco; Blue Willow, Second Revised Edition; Gaston's Blue Willow; Collector's Encyclopedia of Flow Blue China; Collector's Encyclopedia of Flow Blue China, Second Series; Gaston's Flow Blue China, The Comprehensive Guide;* and *English China.*

Preface

My book, *English China*, 2002, focused on the many kinds of decorations used on the various types of china bodies made principally in the Staffordshire district of England during the early 1800s through the first years of the twentieth century. Examples included molded and applied decorations; hand-painted enamel, gilt, and lustre decors; and transfer patterns encompassing a number of different themes such as animal and insect, figural, floral, Oriental, and scenic.

Collections of English china, can be classified or categorized in ways other than by decoration, however. During the nineteenth century, and especially during the Victorian years, table china included numerous pieces for specific uses. Services were not confined to a four-piece place setting with one or two platters and a few serving bowls. Special dishes were made for serving different foods such as asparagus, berries, chestnuts, fish and game, and desserts to name just a few, as well as for several libations such as ale, chocolate, coffee, punch, tea, and wine. Bone dishes, cup plates, meat drainers, sugar shakers, and teapots are just a few such categories. Having written about table china for 25 years, I am still intrigued by pieces which are largely obsolete for today's world of dining or which reflect other aspects of the Victorian era, such as inkwells and hatpin holders.

In this edition, the emphasis is on type of piece, with the particular pattern or decoration being the secondary consideration. A Pattern Index, however, is included for ease in accessing a particular pattern. A Manufacturer's Index, including the patterns and examples made by each and shown in this edition, is also included. Examples are presented in alphabetical order by object, with a brief definition or purpose of the particular item. While the purpose of most pieces is obvious, a number of examples have unusual or unique definitions. The type of decoration is described and the manufacturer is noted, as well as a date denoting the approximate time when the piece was made. Dating is based on information from Geoffrey A. Godden's *Encyclopedia of British Pottery and Porcelain Marks*, 1964.

One to several to many examples are shown for a category of objects, depending upon its varied characteristics. For example, a large number of teapots is included because of the different shapes and decorations they exhibit. There is only one "comb holder," for it is a relatively rare item. Abundant examples are available for bowls, plates, and platters, but those pieces have been included here only if they are decorated by a pattern or décor not shown in my first book. Over 500 photographs illustrate *English China Patterns & Pieces*. Some examples from *English China*, 2002, have been included in addition to many new pieces. A number of items from my other books, *Blue Willow* and *Flow Blue China*, are also shown, allowing for a broader scope in this new survey of English china. A value range for each example is included.

Historically, and to this day, the heart of the English china industry is the Staffordshire district of England. Staffordshire is located in the north central part of the island, composed of small towns which have been engaged in making china since the middle 1600s. From primitive beginnings, the English china industry developed and prospered. The availability both of clays, suitable for making china, and coal, which was needed to fire the ovens, were the underlying reasons why the English china industry became concentrated in the Staffordshire area. The discovery of the underglaze transfer printing process and accessible routes of transportation for shipping finished products are major reasons why that industry thrived. Because of the prolific exporting of English china to America during the 1800s to the present, plus the wide range of pieces and decorations that were made, English china comprises a large part of the collectible china market in the United States.

In my earlier book, I discussed three major elements to consider when collecting English china: ceramic body type, decoration, and manufacturers and their marks. These three elements are, of course, interrelated, and one element may take precedence over another, depending on the particular area of specialization. Some collections are composed of a certain body type, such as majolica or parian. Other collections may be based on the assorted or specific type of production of a manufacturer, such as any china made by Josiah Wedgwood, or only Wedgwood's Jasper Ware. Decoration, of course, is usually the primary focal point for a collector. Although objects are the format for this edition, decoration, body type, and manufacturer are equally important. A closer examination of those three elements, body types, decoration, and manufacturer's marks, follows to provide a basic introduction to ceramics in general and English china in particular.

I hope you enjoy the interesting and unique dimensions of English china presented here.

Mary Frank Gaston
P. O. Box 342, Bryan, TX 77806

Collectors' Glossary for English China

Ceramic Body Types

English china was manufactured in all three body types common to the china industry. These include earthenwares, stonewares, and porcelain, both soft paste and hard paste. A brief discussion of each makes it possible to understand the differences among these ceramic body types.

Earthenwares are made from many different types of natural clays, including kaolin, ball clay, and Cornish stone. Earthenware is fired at temperatures below 1,200°C. If a glaze is applied, the object is re-fired at a temperature below 1,100°C. Earthenware is opaque, that is, you cannot see through it. Technically, earthenware is a type of pottery which has a porosity of more than five percent. Earthenwares may be waterproof if they are covered with a glaze. The glaze, however, is separate from the clay body. The glaze and body are not fused together completely during the glaze (second) firing. Consequently, earthenwares are the weakest of the three ceramic body types. Majolica is an example of glazed earthenware. A clay flower pot is an example of unglazed earthenware.

Stoneware is made from natural clays which are of a sedimentary type and are fined grained and quite plastic. Stoneware differs from simple earthenware in that it has a porosity of less than five percent because stoneware is fired at extremely high temperatures ranging from 1,200 to 1,400°C. A glaze is applied to the earthenware body before the first firing, and during that first firing, the body and the glaze fuse together and become vitrified, that is, like glass. Additional glazes can be added to stoneware bodies after the first firing, but they are not necessary because the vitreous quality is achieved during the first firing. Stoneware, like earthenware, is opaque, but stoneware is heavier than earthenware. Stoneware is also harder and more durable. Basalt, ironstone, and certain types of crockery are examples of stoneware.

Porcelain, the third type of ceramic body, is actually considered to be a special type of stoneware. That is because porcelain is also fired to a state of vitrification. Stoneware, however, is not fired to a state of translucency as porcelain is. Porcelain objects are first fired at temperatures around 900°C. After this first firing, the object is translucent, but it is not vitreous. The translucent quality is obtained from the type of ingredients used in making the body paste. After the first firing, the resulting product is called bisque or biscuit, meaning unglazed. Figurines are examples of porcelain which are often found with bisque or unglazed bodies. To attain vitreosity, the object must be baked a second time with a glaze and re-fired at temperatures of 1,300 to 1,500°C. Porcelain differs from the other two body types, earthenware and stoneware, in that it is translucent, and that is the reason why it has become common to differentiate china into three body types. Porcelain is also lighter in weight than stoneware and is stronger or more durable than earthenware.

Porcelain, moreover, is divided into three types: bone paste, soft paste, and hard paste. The paste type depends on the type and percentage of basic ingredients used as well as the manufacturing process. All three types are translucent in both the bisque and glazed states. They are light in weight, but are still strong. They are also vitreous, if glazed.

Bone paste (or bone china) was so called because its principal ingredient was made of an ash made from calcined animal bones. This bone ash constitutes at least 50 percent of the paste with such materials as china clay and feldspar making up the rest of the formula. Bone paste is stronger than soft paste porcelain, and the manufacturing process is also less expensive. The product is first fired, unglazed, to a translucent state at a temperature of over 1,200°C. It is fired a second time with the glaze at a lower temperature, below 1,100°C. The Spode, Worcester, and Wedgwood factories introduced bone china in England during the latter part of the 1700s and early 1800s. England is still the center for this type of production, although manufacturing processes have been modernized.

Soft paste porcelain refers to the degree of temperature needed for the firing process, which is lower than the temperatures required for firing bone paste and hard paste porcelain. Soft paste porcelain is not actually "soft." Objects are first fired at about 1,100°C. After the glaze is applied, the object is re-fired at a lower temperature. Due to the lower glaze-firing temperatures, soft paste porcelain is not as durable as bone paste or hard paste. English factories such as Bow and Chelsea made soft paste porcelain during the 1700s.

Hard paste porcelain is considered to be a natural porcelain because its ingredients exist in the earth. That was not the case with bone china which used ash from animal bones in the paste or the early soft paste mixtures which used glass in the paste. Kaolin, a type of earth containing hydrated aluminum silicates, accounts for 50 percent of the hard paste mixture. Feldspar is the other important natural ingredient. Feldspar comes from a rock, and it is necessary not only for the body paste but also for the body glaze.

Feldspar adds strength to the paste, allowing the object to be fired at a high temperature and to become translucent. The glaze contains a larger percentage of feldspar than the body paste. It also contains quartz which is necessary for the glaze and paste to melt together and fuse into one entity. The object is then vitreous or like glass. Hard paste objects are first fired at around 900°C. The second firing with the glaze is at temperatures of from 1,400 to 1,600°C. Most European hard paste porcelain, historically, has been produced in Germany, France, and Austria. Although a few English factories, such as Bristol, made hard paste porcelain, English china is primarily found with earthenware, stoneware, or bone china bodies.

English Ceramic Bodies, Types, and Terms

Basalt – a black, unglazed stoneware with a matte finish of Egyptian origin, but Josiah Wedgwood gained renown for this type of ware in English ceramics during the latter part of the eighteenth century.

Biscuit – items made of clay, earthenwares, or porcelains, which have been fired only once and are unglazed.

Bisque – unglazed china, a term usually applied to hard paste porcelain.

Bone China – a translucent china incorporating bone ash in the paste. Bone china is the principal type of china made in England.

Ceramic – items composed of clay and fired at high temperatures.

China – popularly refers to any kind of ceramic body, but the word technically is meant only for hard paste porcelain.

Crazing – a network of lines visible on the surface of a glazed earthenware body caused by the clay body and glaze not being fused completely together during the firing process.

Cream Ware or Queen's Ware – an earthenware body, covered with a clear tin glaze, which was quite durable and a light yellow or "cream" in color. Josiah Wedgwood introduced this ware circa 1760. He named it "Queen's Ware," for Queen Charlotte after he received her patronage in 1765.

Crockery – utilitarian pottery generally made of earthenware.

Earthenware – technically means one of the two classes of pottery, and has a porosity of more than five percent. Earthenwares are composed of various types of natural clays and fired at high temperatures. They are opaque and not vitreous, although they may be glazed. Because earthenwares are not vitreous even when glazed, the surface can be penetrated. This accounts for the "crazing" or network of lines often visible on earthenware bodies.

Fired – to bake clay-formed items at high temperatures.

Hard Paste – a translucent type of porcelain, made of kaolin and feldspar, which is vitreous if glazed.

Ironstone – a type of stoneware incorporating ground iron slag with the clay mixture resulting in a hard body with a shiny finish which is opaque and very durable. Ironstone was patented in England by the Mason company in 1813. Other companies made similar wares but used different names to describe them such as granite ware and stone china.

Jasper Ware – a type of unglazed white stoneware, containing barium sulphate, introduced by Josiah Wedgwood circa 1774. Wedgwood discovered that colors could be added to the paste, resulting in colored bodies. Later the white stoneware was dipped in color rather than having the color incorporated with the clay mixture.

Majolica – an earthenware with a special glaze containing tin. The body is brown in color but is decorated with monochrome or polychrome glazes. Molded and relief work on the body are also typical. Minton is responsible for introducing this type of ware in England about 1850, but majolica's origins are several hundred years earlier, originating in Italy, and called *faience*.

Mold or Mould – a form made in a desired shape to hold the clay paste and thus give form to an object.

Opaque – meaning that light does not pass through the object, the opposite of translucent.

Paneled – refers to ceramic bodies which are molded with definite angular sides rather than being totally round in shape.

Parian – an unglazed hard paste porcelain made to imitate marble. Parian was well adapted to creating busts and figures and other decorative objects. Several English factories made this type of body from the mid 1800s, after it was introduced by Copeland, in 1846 (Boger, p. 256).

Paste – the basic clay mixture of any china before it is shaped and formed.

Porcelain – technically a form of stoneware because it is fired to a vitreous state. Porcelain is distinguished from stoneware, however, because porcelain is translucent. The term porcelain is used to designate true or hard paste porcelain whose principal ingredient is kaolin, a type of clay containing hydrated aluminum silicates. Little true porcelain was made in England.

Pottery – objects formed from clay and fired at high temperatures. The two major categories of pottery are earthenwares and stonewares.

Redware – a red clay earthenware.

Semi-Porcelain – china with a glazed body, but not translucent and not totally vitreous.

Semi-Vitreous – not completely vitreous, that is, it is neither waterproof, nor like glass.

Soft Paste – a type of porcelain fired at lower temperatures in its second firing than is the case for hard paste porcelain.

Spur or Stilt Marks – small protrusions usually found in three places on either the back or front of a piece of china which was caused by the clay supports which were used to separate objects in the kiln during the firing process.

Stone China – properly refers to the stoneware body introduced by Spode, circa 1805, which had a brilliant glazed surface, was opaque, hard, heavy, and durable. The term "stone china," however, evolved as a name used by other English manufacturers for china similar to Spode's or to Mason's ironstone china.

Stoneware or Stone Ware – technically the second major classification of pottery. Stonewares have a porosity of less than five percent because feldspar and quartz are added to the clay mixture causing the body to become vitrified when fired at a high temperature during the first firing. Stonewares are not fired to a state of translucency, however, and thus are opaque.

Terra Cotta – red clay earthenware which is not glazed, like a flower pot.

Vitreous – impervious to liquids, like glass. Stonewares and porcelains are completely vitreous because the glaze and the body are fired together until they fuse together to form one entity. Thus the outer glaze cannot be penetrated.

Decorations

Decoration on English china is usually divided into transfer decoration and non-transfer decoration. Although a large percentage of English china represents transfer decoration, non-transfer decoration was used on many types of collectible English china. Non-transfer decoration encompasses a variety of methods and is by no means limited to hand-painted themes which are the obvious opposite of transfer decoration. In fact, non-transfer decoration can be roughly divided into two kinds, unpainted and painted.

Unpainted decoration relates totally to the body of the china where some form of decoration is made directly on the china body or applied to the body before it is fired. Very simple to quite complicated decoration can be achieved by different methods. Examples include molded relief or intaglio designs, machine turned or incised work, and the application of other materials or separate molded decoration affixed to the body of the china. Flowers and leaves created separately in a realistic image and applied to a vase or a pitcher are examples of applied décor. Applied decoration can also refer to something added to the entire body of an object, such as salt added during the glaze firing to create a special effect of a pitted surface on the ceramic body. Such unpainted decoration enables the surface of the china to be further decorated by painting or other methods.

For non-transfer decorations, the application of color is by hand. The color can take various forms such as enamel and gilt and can be applied either before or after an object is fired or before or after an object is glazed, depending on the type of decoration desired. Colored enamel glazes, resist applied lustres, and hand-painted decorative themes are some examples of this form of non-transfer decoration. Hand-painted work ranges from simple lines and sponged-on color, to floral designs, to full portraits or scenes.

Transfer ware may be considered synonymous with English china because historically so much china was decorated by that method, and transfer wares make up a very large part of the American collectible English china market. The "Willow" pattern is probably the best known example of a transfer pattern. Transfer decoration is also called lithography. In lithography, a design is etched on a stone or a copper plate. The design is then filled in with ink, and a thin piece of paper is pressed onto the design. The paper with the imprint of the design is then "transferred" to a piece of pottery. Any of the three types of ceramic bodies can be decorated with a transfer pattern.

The transfer method of decoration has been in use in England since about 1750. In the beginning, transfers were first applied over the glaze on the china body and then touched up or painted entirely. The overglaze transfers could become worn off, however, and were not totally satisfactory as a form of decoration. It was not until about 1760 that the underglaze transfer printing process was successful. Underglaze hand-painted decoration had been used in China for hundreds of years. The Chinese had discovered that the color blue, derived from the mineral cobalt, was the one color which could withstand the high degrees of heat necessary to fire the glaze and still maintain clarity of the design under the glaze. That is why Oriental porcelains were decorated with blue. The English, wanting to emulate the Chinese style, designs, and colors, also found it was necessary to use the color blue for underglaze decoration. The underglaze decoration was permanent, and the process revolutionized the china decorating industry in England. It not only made decoration easier and less expensive, but it allowed for a number of items to be decorated with the same design. By the mid-1800s, other underglaze colors, such as black, brown, and mulberry were perfected. Later, multicolored underglaze transfers were possible.

Terms relating to the types of decoration which are found on examples in this book and frequently found in relation to English ceramics are briefly defined next. These terms do not describe the components of particular patterns but rather a method of decoration or a general category of

decoration. For instance, "transfer printing" is the term for a particular method of decoration, and it also is a general category of decoration, "transfer ware." The "willow" pattern is an example of a transfer decoration and an example of transfer ware as well. The particular rendition of that pattern by different companies is not always the same, however. In the descriptions of those examples, the pattern will be noted not just as "willow," but as a type of willow pattern, such as Traditional or Burleigh or Canton. For detailed descriptions of the various willow patterns, please see *Gaston's Blue Willow*, 2004. Similarly, cameo ware is both a method of decoration and a general collecting category. The Josiah Wedgwood factory is famous for cameo decoration, but there are many decoration themes or patterns.

Decorating Methods and Types

ABC Ware — children's china, usually plates, decorated with letters of the alphabet around the outer border, with a center pattern of animals or themes and characters from nursery rhymes.

Applied — any decoration which is formed separately and then affixed to a ceramic body.

Bas-relief — low relief work where the decoration does not stand out very much from the body of the china.

Basketweave — a ceramic body decoration where the clay has either been woven by hand or molded with a pattern to resemble a woven basket.

Bat Printing — a transfer technique of decorating china used during the late 1700s. A "bat" of glue picked up the engraved design from the copper plate and then the "bat" with the design was transferred to a ceramic body. This particular type of transfer is characterized by a stippled design which is then dusted with a colored powder. The object is then fired to melt the colored powder and to set the decoration.

Brush Stroke — a term used to refer to some hand-painted decoration, typically associated with hand-painted Flow Blue patterns.

Cameo Ware — relief decoration molded separately and then affixed to a ceramic body. The cameos are made of the same material as the body of the piece, but the relief work is left uncolored or with a natural white finish.

Chelsea Grape China — white ceramic bodies decorated with fruit or floral designs in low relief with a lavender-blue finish, often accented or covered with a copper lustre.

Chinoiserie — decorations with an Oriental motif.

Chintz China — a polychrome floral transfer pattern which covers the entire surface of a piece of china.

Cobalt Blue — a color used to decorate ceramics which was derived from an oxide of the mineral, cobalt. The substance

is brown in color when it is applied to the ceramic body, but the high heat during the firing process transforms the color to a deep blue.

Combed — a hand-painted decorating technique of "combing" color over a ceramic body to produce a mottled or marbled effect, used from the 1600s.

Commemorative China — decoration depicting a specific person, date, event, or place.

Crested Ware — china decorated with a crest or a coat of arms, commissioned by families or other entities. Plates as well as other items such as beakers, loving cups, and mugs are found with this type of decoration.

Daubed — a hand-painted decorating technique of "daubing" color randomly on a ceramic body.

Dipped — a term used to refer to coating a ceramic body with a colored glaze.

Enamel — colors composed of glass and various minerals used to decorate ceramics. The glass gives a vitreous quality and shiny look while the color depends on the particular mineral used in the glass mixture. Colored enamels may be applied to a glazed or unglazed ceramic body. The object must then be re-fired to set the color.

Flow Blue — a decorating technique used chiefly on underglaze blue transfer ware. This method originated in Staffordshire from the late 1820s. By adding certain chemicals such as saltpetre, borax, and white lead to the kiln during the glaze firing, the cobalt blue color used for the underglaze pattern would "run," obscuring the detailed lines of the design, resulting in a smudged, flowing effect.

Gaudy — refers to brightly colored hand-painted polychrome enamel decorations heavily applied over a pattern, found on earthenware or stoneware bodies. The colors reflect the influence of the Japanese Imari wares which were painted with cobalt blue and burnt orange. While gaudy decoration was hand painted, sometimes the colors were applied over transfer designs. This re-inforced the term, "gaudy," because the paint obscured the lines of the design, resulting in a colorful, but uneven look.

Gaudy Dutch – primitive floral patterns painted in a large and bold manner using the Imari colors of cobalt blue and burnt orange. The cobalt blue was applied over the glaze.

Gaudy Ironstone – decorated in various colors in a gaudy style.

Gaudy Welsh – cobalt blue applied underglaze in panels and accented with burnt orange over the glaze, like Imari décor.

Gilding – to decorate with gold.

Glazes – the liquid, glassy substance which is applied to ceramics to make them impervious to liquids, and also used in various colors to decorate ceramics.

Grandmother Ware – see Chelsea Grape China.

Hand Painted – refers to colored decoration applied by hand to china. Hand-painted decoration can be either over or under the glaze. Early transfer designs were filled in or accented with hand-painted work.

Hand Tinted – transfer designs filled in with light or soft shades of color, not bold or vivid.

Imari Colors – a Japanese decoration using cobalt blue as an underglaze color with a burnt-orange overglaze design, similar to Gaudy décor.

India Red – a burnt-orange color.

Jackfield – a red earthenware with a black glaze.

Japan Colors – cobalt blue and burnt-orange decoration found on Mason Ironstone.

Japonaise – decoration emulating the Japanese style.

Intaglio – a molded body design which is concave rather than convex.

Lustres or Lusters – a metallic finish on ceramic bodies achieved by applying a coating, or design, composed of a particular metal or mineral, such as copper, which is reduced during the firing process until only the metal remains as the decoration. Lustres are found in a variety of colors including gold, pink, purple, and silver, depending on the substance used.

Machine Turned – designs on ceramics formed by machine rather than by hand.

Marbled – mottled glazes on ceramics made by "combing" the color over the body surface.

Mat or Matte – a finish which is dull, not glossy.

Monochrome – decoration on china composed of just one color on the ceramic body. Monochrome can actually refer to a colored glaze over all of the body or a pattern or design in just one color over the white body; the blue willow pattern is a monochrome blue on white decoration.

Motto Ware – pottery decorated with writing, such as verses, maxims, or mottos, made in the Torquay area of South Devon from the late 1800s. The words were incised through the glaze, exposing the red clay of the ceramic body,

thus achieving a contrast in decoration between the words and colored glaze.

Mulberry – a dark brown to dark purple color used for English underglaze transfer patterns from the 1830s to 1850s.

Openwork – body decoration where the clay is shaped to have a pierced rather than solid design, usually found around the border of an object.

Overglaze – any decoration applied on top of the glazed ceramic body.

Pâte sur Pâte – paste on paste, an applied relief form body decoration made by applying layers of liquid slip until the desired shape is obtained. This form of decoration originated in France, but in England, Minton became known for this technique after the company hired a former Sevres artist, Solon, circa 1870.

Polychrome – more than one solid color used to decorate china. The term can refer either to hand-painted or transfer decoration.

Pratt Ware – underglaze polychrome patterns made by William Pratt from circa 1780 to 1799, highlighted by wide borders finished with solid glazes in rich colors.

Relief – ceramic body decoration where the clay body has decoration molded or shaped to stand out from the body in a raised or convex manner.

Reticulated – openwork, or perforated ceramic body decoration.

Resist – refers to a decorating method whereby parts of a design are prevented from receiving color and remain undecorated such as silver and lustre resist wares.

Salt Glaze – an early type of glaze used on English stonewares which has a pitted surface caused by putting salt in the kiln during the firing process.

Sepia – a reddish-brown color used on early transfer patterns.

Slip – a liquid form of clay made with water and used as an early form of decoration on china. The liquid clay was applied by a quill to form designs.

Spattered – decoration made by dusting color on a ceramic body.

Sponged – color decoration applied by using a sponge to daub the color on the body surface.

Sprigged – a term used to describe applied relief decoration, where the decoration is formed separately from the body, then applied to the body and attached using liquid slip.

Sprig Ware – hand-painted décor of very small flowers in polychrome enamels over the glaze, usually found on porcelain or soft paste bodies.

Stick – a hand-painted decoration of lines painted or combed over the body surface.

Tapestry – a form of applied body decoration where a cloth is fired onto the body of the china resulting in a body having the same texture as the cloth. Although the cloth is destroyed during the firing, the imprint of its texture is left.

Transfer Printing — indicates that designs or patterns have been engraved on copper plates, the grooves of the designs filled with ink or paint, after which the copper plate is heated and a soapy tissue paper is pressed into the engraved design, taken off, and in turn pressed upside down on an object which has been heated and coated with varnish and then re-heated so that the pattern will stick. After the object has dried, the paper is washed off, but the design remains — thus the design has been "transferred" from the copper plate to the object. Transfers on ceramics can be applied over or under the glaze.

Transfer Wares — any china decorated with a transfer print, commonly refers to English printed china made during the eighteenth and nineteenth centuries.

Underglaze — decoration applied either by hand painting or transfer to the clay body before the glaze firing. Underglaze decoration is permanent.

Whieldon Ware — a brown, mottled underglaze decoration used by Thomas Whieldon in the mid-to-late eighteenth century.

Marks

Marks on English china are important for collectors so that not only the particular manufacturer can be determined, but also the approximate age of the china. While a large percentage of English china is found with marks, collectors should be aware that many examples are found without marks, especially pieces made prior to 1800. Godden, 1964, notes (Plate Three) that printed marks on English china were not routinely used until after the mid-1700s. Marks on English china were made in several different ways. They were either incised, impressed, hand painted, or printed. The first two methods incorporated the mark into the body of the china before it was fired. Hand-painted marks and printed marks, made from transfers or stamps, were applied before or after the glaze firing of the china. If the marks were applied under the glaze, then the mark became permanent.

Because of Geoffrey Godden's extensive research regarding English ceramic marks, collectors of English china are easily able to identify and date most English marks with the assistance of his books, particularly the *Encyclopedia of British Pottery and Porcelain Marks,* 1964. Many of the English factories maintained precise marking systems which included not only the name of the pottery, but the month and year of production, the inventory or design number, and often an artist's mark. Tables are available to interpret such marks for companies like Minton, Royal Crown Derby, Wedgwood, and Worcester to name a few.

Knowledge of several general facts about English marks is also useful, and a number of these are listed below. A few misconceptions, however, are common regarding English marks. One concerns English registry marks which have been used since 1842. An impressed or printed diamond symbol with letters and numbers, or just printed numbers prefaced with the initials "RD," are sometimes found on English china. These marks indicate that the pattern or mold of the object was registered with the British Patent Office in order to keep that particular pattern or mold from being copied by another manufacturer. Godden (1964, pp. 526 – 528) has printed tables for decoding the marks and numbers which can identify specific years. General books on marks also usually contain these tables. The registry marks are often misinterpreted, mistakenly thought to mean that if a piece has such a mark, that the particular piece was made in that particular year which corresponds to the registry number. The numbers only refer to when the design or shape was first patented. The same design or shape could have been used during many subsequent years, maintaining the original registry mark. Designs or shapes might also have been used prior to their registration. Also not all china made after 1842 bears a registry mark. The registry marks are useful primarily as a clue only to the period when the pattern or shape was first invented.

Another error regarding English ceramic marks may be caused by marks which include a printed year. The designation of a year with a mark usually only indicates the year when the factory was first founded, often many, even hundreds, of years prior to when the piece bearing the year mark was made. The factory may have changed ownership several times and may not even have the original name. It was a common practice of ceramic factories, not only in England, but in other European countries, especially during the late nineteenth and early twentieth centuries, to incorporate founding dates with their later marks.

The name "Wedgwood" can be misinterpreted when found as a mark on English china. Several companies used this name in their marks. The most famous Wedgwood company is the Josiah Wedgwood firm which was founded in 1759. His marks are not spelled with an "e" (Wedgewood) nor do they include the initial "J.," or "& Co." William Smith marked china with "Wedgewood" (with an "e") after 1848 until 1855 (Godden, 1964, p. 583). Godden (1964, p. 687) states that a John Wedge Wood operated a pottery from 1841 to 1860 and used a mark that incorporated the name "J. Wedgwood." "Wedgwood" was also used by Podmore, Walker & Co. who eventually changed the company name to Wedgwood & Co. circa 1860. Enoch Wedgwood was the Wedgwood associated with that company, and thus the basis for that company's use of the name (see Godden, 1964, pp. 501, 655). Collectors should realize that Wedgwood marked china made by these other companies is still collectible, but such pieces should not be attributed to the Josiah Wedgwood company.

Marks on modern reproductions present another point of confusion for collectors. Historically, ceramic marks have been copied, and often such later copies are collectible today because they are still old and desirable. Today the collectible china market is heavily stocked with a large assortment of new china designed, and often marked, to replicate the old. Some of the current reproductions of English china include majolica, Staffordshire figures, "flow blue," and the blue willow pattern as well as other scenic or "romantic" transfer designs. Some of the china with "misleading" English marks has been around for over 20 years. It is understandable how new collectors might not be aware of or alert to those reproductions. Some of the china is not marked, but other examples often include a coat of arms mark printed with "Victoria" and "Ironstone Staffordshire England." This china has been made since the late 1960s by Blakeney Pottery Limited which is located in Stoke-on-Trent. Another mark used by the firm is

composed of a large floral cartouche and includes the words "Romantic" and "Flo Blue, T. M. Staffordshire, England." The company specializes in Victorian reproductions. Mustache cups, shaving mugs, footbaths, bowl and pitcher sets, and cheese keepers are just a few of the items they produce.

There are a few general rules of thumb to remember regarding modern reproductions. Always be wary of any illegible mark. Some genuine marks, especially on flow blue china, are smudged, but today some marks are deliberately blurred. "Flo Blue" was never printed on china decorated with the special technique that turned out to be the highly collectible "Flow Blue" china. Authentic Staffordshire figures are generally unmarked. Large offerings of the same pattern of similar Victorian type objects at flea markets and other antique outlets usually are a good indication that the china is new. Prices can also reflect new china. If the prices are low, such as $25.00 for a cheese keeper, almost unquestionably the piece is new. Unfortunately, though, prices which genuinely old items would fetch are found on many new examples. When paying large prices for any collectible or antique item, a careful collector would demand a money-back guarantee if the item is later found to be a reproduction.

English Ceramic Marks, Types, and Terms

"England" is found in some English marks from the last quarter of the nineteenth century, but was used on all exported wares after 1891 to comply with American tariff laws.

Garter marks are printed marks, round or oval in shape, used by some English factories during the latter half of the nineteenth century.

Impressed marks are made in the form of initials or symbols and pressed into the ceramic body before it is fired.

Incised marks are cut into the ceramic body before it is fired.

Limited (Ltd.) is a word or abbreviation found in many English marks after 1880.

"Made In England" is noted by most authorities to definitely be of twentieth century origin. "Made in," and the particular country name, is noted by the Kovels (p. 231) to have been required by English law on imported wares from 1887. But no specific requirement is noted for china exported from England or for china imported by the United States. Therefore "Made in" as part of a mark on English china does not indicate any specific year. Thus some examples from the same historical period may have this mark and others will not.

Overglaze describes marks placed on an object after it has been glazed. Overglaze marks are hand painted or printed. Marks applied overglaze can be worn off or taken off.

Pattern names printed with marks were not used before the early 1800s.

Printed marks refer to marks made in the form of a transfer or stamp. Such marks can be applied either over or under the glaze.

Raised marks are those formed in relief on the body of the china before it is fired or formed separately and then affixed to the ceramic body before it is fired.

Registry marks are marks or numbers impressed or printed on English ceramics after 1842. Diamond shaped marks were the first type used and were continued until 1883. After that time, the consecutive numbering system, prefaced with the initials "RD," was used. Tables to decipher such marks are found in general marks books. These registration numbers were assigned to companies in order to protect a shape or pattern design for three years, but the registry marks could continue to be placed on the china after that three year period. When interpreted, these registry letters or numbers will identify the year such designs were first registered. Thus, the registry marks only indicate when the company registered the design, and it is possible that the design was used before it was registered. Many designs were never registered.

"Royal" is a word used in English marks after 1850.

Royal Arms marks are printed marks of coats of arms and were not used before the 1800s.

Staffordshire Knot or Bow Knot refers to a bow-knot shape used to mark English ceramics during the 1880s.

"Trade Mark" is a term used in English marks primarily after the last quarter of the nineteenth century.

Underglaze refers to marks applied to ceramic bodies before they are glazed. Such marks are permanent and cannot be worn or taken off, although, they can be covered over.

Apothecary Jar to Wine Jug

Apothecary Jar, a bottle or jug made of simple earthenware. It was used to hold medicines or tonics concocted by apothecaries (druggists or pharmacists). Jars were printed with names and advertisements for the products.

1. Apothecary Jar, 5½"h, unmarked, circa late 1800s, printed with a trademark, name, and advertisement: "Virol, A Preparation Of Bone Marrow, An Ideal Fat Food For Children & Invalids." $50.00 – 65.00.

2. Apothecary Jar, 5"h, unmarked, circa late 1800s, printed with name and advertisement: "Numol, Tonic and Nervine, Lecithin Food, Body Builder, Digestive and Appetizing for Children & Adults." $50.00 – 65.00.

Ashtray, a receptacle for ashes from cigarettes and cigars, basically a twentieth century item, peaking in popularity and necessity from the 1920s to the 1940s. Although ashtrays are still in use, they are quickly becoming collector items as production diminishes because of fewer smokers! English ashtrays are usually made of earthenware or bone china. Many collectible ones carry some form of advertising. Those made in an Art Deco shape are also in demand.

3. Ashtray, 6"sq, traditional *Willow* pattern, Royal Doulton, circa 1920s. $65.00 – 85.00.

4. ASHTRAY, 4½"d, dark brown transfer floral pattern on border with the crest for the University of Michigan, as indicated by the mark on the back, Josiah Wedgwood, circa 1941. $20.00 – 30.00.

Barber Bottle, used by barbers to store oils and lotions.

Bar Measure, this type of piece was made during the reigns of King George II and King George III (Barber, p. 51, 1914). The stoneware body is salt glazed, decorated with a deep cobalt blue, and bears the initials "GR" over a lightly embossed crest. Examples are rare.

5. BAR MEASURE, 9½"h, unmarked, circa 1760 – 1820. $1,000.00 – 1,200.00.

6. BARBER BOTTLE, 7¼"h, (stopper missing), Jasper Ware, decorated with figures of muses and grapes and leaves in relief on a cobalt glazed body, Josiah Wedgwood, circa 1850. $500.00 – 600.00.

Basket, a deep dish with a top handle, usually large in size, often used to hold fruit.

7. Basket, 8"h, majolica, decorated with a wide cobalt blue border and pink and blue flowers with green leaves in relief, unmarked, circa 1870. $800.00 – 1,000.00.

Beer Bottle, usually made of crockery or stoneware with some type of stopper.

8. Beer Bottle, 7½"h, cork stopper, made by Lovatt & Lovatt, circa late 1890s. "Lovatt" impressed mark on front of bottle at base. "Arnold Perrett & Co., Limited, Home Brew, Ginger Beer," printed in black on front side. $50.00 – 60.00.

Berry Dish, a medium size to large bowl with a perforated top or separate perforated liner to drain water or juice from the fruit. These serving dishes often had matching small bowls for individual servings.

9. Berry Dish and underplate, octagonal shape, Josiah Wedgwood, after 1891. $800.00 – 1,000.00.

10. **BERRY DISH,** Chintz pattern, *Balmoral*, Grimwade's "Royal Winton" line, circa 1930s – 1940s. Note the holes are camouflaged by the pattern. $300.00 – 400.00.

11. **BERRY DISH,** individual size, Flow Blue floral pattern, *Oxford*, Johnson Bros., circa early 1900s. $60.00 – 75.00.

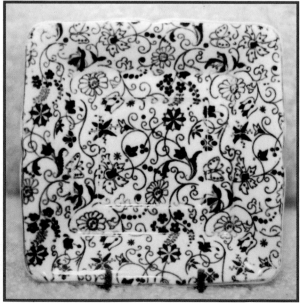

12. **BERRY DISH,** individual size, square shape, overall floral pattern in a chintz style, unmarked, circa mid-to-late 1800s. This type of "chintz" design is not to be confused with "chintz" patterns popular during the 1930s to 1940s and shown in the previous example of a berry bowl. $75.00 – 100.00.

Biscuit Barrel or Jar, dishes for holding cookies, referred to as "biscuits" in England. Examples are usually five to six inches high. They may have a metal rather than a ceramic lid. Some may also have metal bail-type handles. These were a popular English item and were made by many factories with a variety of decorations.

13. BISCUIT BARREL, 5½"h, Jaspar Ware, classical figures in relief, Josiah Wedgwood, circa 1840. $800.00 – 900.00.

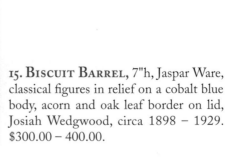

14. BISCUIT BARREL, the body and decoration of this jar are very similar to the preceding piece, but it was made by Wedgwood & Co., Ltd. (not the Josiah Wedgwood factory), circa 1900. $400.00 – 500.00.

15. BISCUIT BARREL, 7"h, Jaspar Ware, classical figures in relief on a cobalt blue body, acorn and oak leaf border on lid, Josiah Wedgwood, circa 1898 – 1929. $300.00 – 400.00.

16. BISCUIT JAR, traditional *Willow* pattern, silver-plated lid and bail, unmarked, circa early to mid-1900s. $250.00 – 275.00.

17. BISCUIT JAR, octagonal shape, *Willow* pattern, cane handle, Gibson & Sons, Ltd., circa 1912 – 1930. $275.00 – 325.00.

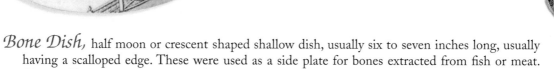

Bone Dish, half moon or crescent shaped shallow dish, usually six to seven inches long, usually having a scalloped edge. These were used as a side plate for bones extracted from fish or meat. Also see Turkey Bone Dish.

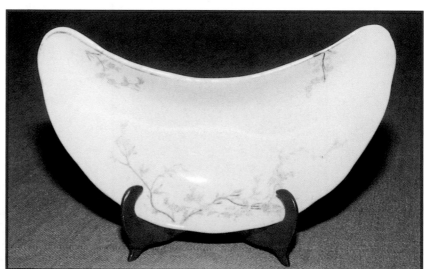

18. BONE DISH, light blue floral pattern, *Blenheim*, T. & R. Boote, Godden Mark 441, circa 1890 – 1906. $30.00 – 40.00.

19. BONE DISH, Flow Blue *Dunbarton* floral pattern, New Wharf Pottery, circa 1890 – 1894. $70.00 – 85.00.

20. BONE DISH, Flow Blue *Martha* floral pattern, Upper Hanley Pottery, circa 1895 – 1900. $75.00 – 100.00.

21. BONE DISH, brown transfer pattern of leaves and berries, *Minerva*, John Edwards, circa 1889. $45.00 – 55.00.

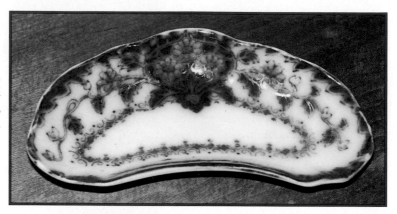

22. BONE DISH, Flow Blue *Seville* floral pattern, Wood & Son, circa 1891 – 1907. $100.00 – 125.00.

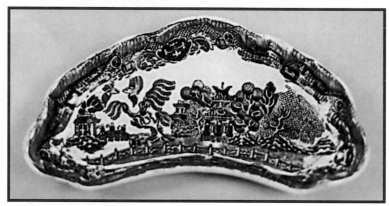

23. BONE DISH, traditional *Willow* pattern, Bourne & Leigh, circa 1892 – 1939. $60.00 – 75.00.

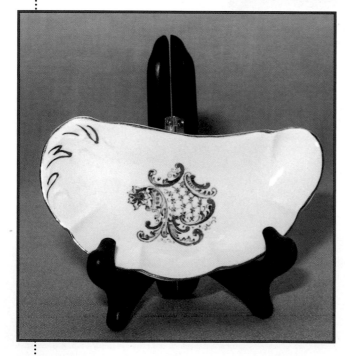

24. BONE DISH, unidentified transfer pattern of scrolled designs with flowers, John Edwards, circa late 1800s. $30.00 – 40.00.

Bread Plate, shallow dishes for serving bread, about 12 inches in diameter or length. These may be found in various shapes: round, oval, or rectangular. The rectangular ones usually have handles and sometimes are referred to as trays. Also see Tray.

25. BREAD PLATE, large peony-like floral pattern in a Flow Blue style covers the interior, unmarked, circa early 1900s. $100.00 – 125.00.

26. BREAD PLATE, majolica decorated with green leaves and small pink flowers on a bright yellow ground, unmarked, circa 1870. $600.00 – 700.00.

Bulb Bowl, a shallow bowl used as a planter for growing flower bulbs indoors.

27. BULB BOWL, multicolored *Willow* pattern with lustre enhancement, S. Fielding & Co., see Godden Mark 1548, circa 1917 – 1930. $300.00 – 350.00.

28. Bulb Bowl, 12"d, brightly colored enameled decoration of a bird, insect, grapes, and leaves on a white ground, Wileman & Co. with a Registry Number for 1919. $275.00 – 325.00.

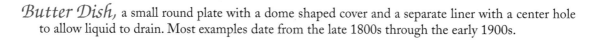

Butter Dish, a small round plate with a dome shaped cover and a separate liner with a center hole to allow liquid to drain. Most examples date from the late 1800s through the early 1900s.

29. Butter Dish, Flow Blue *Limoges* pattern, Wood & Son, circa 1891 – 1907. $400.00 – 500.00.

30. Butter Dish, blue and white floral and scroll pattern, *Ormonde*, A. Meakin Ltd., circa 1891 – 1907. $300.00 – 400.00.

31. Liner from *Ormonde* butter dish.

32. Butter Dish, slate blue transfer pattern, *Swallow with Bow*, Brown-Westhead, Moore & Co., circa late 1800s. $350.00 – 450.00.

33. Butter Dish, traditional *Willow* pattern on cover and liner, Ridgways, circa 1927 and after. $350.00 – 400.00.

Butter Pat, small dishes, round or square, approximately three inches in diameter, used for individual servings of butter, or a "pat" of butter.

34. Butter Pats, brown transfer ware: left, *Tournay* pattern, T. & R. Boote, with a Registry Mark for 1885, $25.00 – 30.00; right, un-marked, $12.00 – 15.00 (mc).

35. Butter Pats, brown transfer ware: left, vase with flowers in the foreground and a scenic view in the distance, unmarked ex-cept for a Registry Mark for 1886, $30.00 – 35.00; right, unidentified pattern composed of two large birds flying over a scenic view of water and a village, F. Primavesi & Son, Wales, circa 1860 and after. $35.00 – 40.00.

Cake Plate, two handled dishes, 10 to 12 inches wide, often square rather than round in shape, intended for serving small tea cakes.

36. CAKE PLATE, *Chelsea Grape* enameled pattern, unmarked, circa 1830s. $30.00 – 40.00.

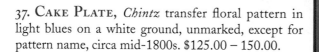

37. CAKE PLATE, *Chintz* transfer floral pattern in light blues on a white ground, unmarked, except for pattern name, circa mid-1800s. $125.00 – 150.00.

38. CAKE PLATE, Flow Blue Oriental figural and scenic pattern, *Kremlin*, Samuel Alcock, circa 1830 – 1859. $400.00 – 500.00.

39. CAKE PLATE, Oriental floral pattern enameled in Japan colors, Mason's "Fenton Stone Works" mark in blue with number "306," circa 1825. $250.00 – 300.00.

40. CAKE PLATE, *Newclus* transfer border pattern composed of reserves of pink flowers on a cobalt blue band, Sampson Smith, circa 1925 – 1930. $75.00 – 90.00.

41. CAKE PLATE, *Trentham,* polychrome enameled center pattern of a floral urn on a cream ground, Josiah Wedgwood, circa 1891 – 1897. $100.00 – 125.00.

42. CAKE PLATE, enameled *Sprig* design of small pink flowers and green leaves, unmarked, circa early 1800s. $40.00 – 45.00.

Cake Stand, a large plate, approximately 12 inches in diameter, with a short, wide pedestal base, designed for holding a whole cake.

43. CAKE STAND, underglaze polychrome Prattware design of an English factory scene with a Greek figural border, unmarked, circa 1850. $400.00 – 450.00.

44. CAKE STAND, Flow Blue *Cleopatra* pattern, unmarked except for pattern name, but attributed to E. Walley, circa mid-1800s. $800.00 – 1,000.00.

45. CAKE STAND, blue and white transfer pattern, *Delph*, unmarked, but the pattern is the same one as *Delft* by Mintons, circa late 1800s. $350.00 – 400.00.

46. CAKE STAND, traditional *Willow* pattern, unmarked, circa mid-1800s. $350.00 – 400.00.

Candleholder, usually made in pairs for the dining table or as part of a dresser set; sometimes referred to as candle sticks. Also see Dresser Set.

47. CANDLEHOLDERS, Flow Blue traditional *Willow* pattern, Doulton, circa 1891 – 1902. $400.00 – 500.00 pair.

48. CANDLEHOLDERS, Jasper Ware, figures in relief of Apollo with lyre and Urania with globe and staff on a cobalt blue dipped ground, Josiah Wedgwood, circa 1840 – 1870. $600.00 – 700.00.

Candle Snuffer, designed to extinguish a candle's fire. The example shown is a figural one, but snuffers were also made in less elaborate forms.

49. **CANDLE SNUFFER,** 3"h, Staffordshire figure of a young boy in colorful dress with a black tri-cornered hat, attributed to Minton, circa 1795. $1,000.00 – 1,200.00.

Centerpiece Bowl, a decorative bowl for fruit or flowers for table or mantel use. These bowls often were made with a pair of matching candleholders.

50. **CENTERPIECE BOWL,** Art Deco stepped shape with a hand-painted stylized floral design, Myott, Son & Co, circa 1920s to 1930s. $125.00 – 150.00.

Chamber Pot, designed as a convenience for the chamber (bedroom), chamber pots were made in sets with other matching toiletry pieces. Lids were made for the pots, but few have survived the years. Also see Wash Set.

51. **CHAMBER POT,** serpent shaped handle, *Peking Japan* pattern, black transfer design painted with burnt orange, blue, and green, Ashworth, circa 1862. $500.00 – 600.00.

52. CHAMBER POT, serpent shaped handle, *Hizen* cobalt blue and white transfer pattern, Ashworth, circa 1862. $400.00 – 500.00.

53. CHAMBER POT, serpent shaped handle, Flow Blue *Iris* pattern, Ashworth, after 1862. $300.00 – 400.00.

54. CHAMBER POT, Art Nouveau floral pattern, *Stratford*, in deep cobalt blue, gold accents, Burgess & Leigh, circa early 1900s. $400.00 – 500.00.

55. CHAMBER POT, Flow Blue traditional *Willow* pattern, Doulton, circa 1891 – 1902. $350.00 – 450.00.

Chamber Stick, a short candleholder made with a handle for carrying and a saucer to catch the melting tallow, typically used to light a path to the bed.

56. CHAMBER STICK, traditional *Willow* pattern, Gibson & Sons, circa 1912 – 1930. $175.00 – 200.00.

57. CHAMBER STICK, 2¾"h, Jaspar Ware decorated with classical figures in relief on a deep cobalt blue ground, Josiah Wedgwood, circa 1910. $275.00 – 325.00.

Cheese Keeper, a rectangular or wedge shaped dish with a cover and a handle on top, to keep cheese fresh. Also see Stilton Cheese Dish.

58. CHEESE KEEPER, Flow Blue *Gainsborough* floral and scroll pattern, Ridgways, circa early 1900s. $550.00 – 650.00.

59. CHEESE KEEPER, Flow Blue *Mandarin* Oriental scenic pattern, Wiltshaw & Robinson, circa early 1900s. $350.00 – 400.00.

60. CHEESE KEEPER, *Burleigh Willow* pattern, Burgess & Leigh, circa 1930s. $325.00 – 375.00.

61. CHEESE KEEPER, floral pattern with deep cobalt blue accents, ornate handle, Doulton, circa early 1900s. $500.00 – 600.00.

62. CHEESE KEEPER, simplified scenic pattern in blue and white, Woodsware, Wood & Sons, circa mid-twentieth century. $100.00 – 125.00.

63. CHEESE KEEPER, Jaspar Ware, classical figures in relief on a cobalt ground decorate the lid which has a silver-plated underplate, Josiah Wedgwood, circa 1840. $600.00 – 700.00.

64. CHEESE KEEPER, Royal Commemorative for the Coronation of Queen Elizabeth II, Sandland Ware, Lancaster & Sandland Ltd., circa 1952. $125.00 – 150.00.

Chestnut Bowl, a reticulated or open work bowl or basket for holding hot chestnuts. These bowls usually have a matching underplate.

65. CHESTNUT BOWL WITH UNDERPLATE, Mason's *Blue Pheasants* pattern, G. M. & C. J. Mason, circa 1820s. $1,800.00 – 2,000.00.

66. CHESTNUT BOWL, traditional *Willow* pattern, unmarked, circa early 1800s. $1,000.00 – 1,200.00.

67. CHESTNUT BOWL, traditional *Willow* pattern, unmarked, circa early 1800s. $1,000.00 – 1,200.00.

Children's China, an assortment of dishes made in small sizes for children's use and also for play, such as tea sets or small versions of serving china like tureens and platters. Popular decorations included themes from nursery rhymes. Alphabet or "ABC" china became an early learning tool as plates displayed the alphabet as a border on many examples.

68. CHILDREN'S CHINA, ABC ware, cup and saucer decorated with a polychrome transfer of little girls, W. Adams & Co., circa 1891 – 1896. $125.00 – 150.00.

69. CHILDREN'S CHINA, ABC ware, plate decorated with a kitten portrait, W. Adams & Co., circa 1896 – 1914. $125.00 – 150.00.

70. CHILDREN'S CHINA, ABC ware, polychrome transfer, "Going to Market," unmarked, circa late 1800s. $120.00 – 140.00.

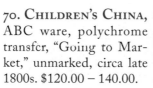

71. Children's China, ABC ware, polychrome farm scene, unmarked, circa late 1800s. $120.00 – 140.00.

72. Children's China, ABC ware, polychrome scenic design, entitled, "Oriental Hotel," unmarked. $120.00 – 140.00.

73. Children's China, ABC ware, blue and white transfer of "Fox and Grapes," a theme based on Aesop's Fables, W. Adams & Co., circa 1896 – 1914. $100.00 – 125.00.

74. CHILDREN'S CHINA, polychrome transfer of boys playing cricket with a rhyme printed around the inner border, unmarked, circa mid to late 1800s. $125.00 – 150.00.

75. CHILDREN'S CHINA, cup, saucer, and covered sugar bowl to a child's tea set, *Mandarin Willow* pattern in pink, Copeland, circa late 1800s. $80.00 – 100.00 each.

76. CHILDREN'S CHINA, platter to a set of toy dishes, *Simplified Willow* pattern, Edge, Malkin & Co., circa 1872 – 1903. $120.00 – 140.00.

77. CHILDREN'S CHINA, soup bowl from a child's set of dishes, blue and white scenic transfer, part of the "Old Curiosity Shop" line by Ridgways, based on scenes from Charles Dickens, circa early 1900s (see Williams II, p. 100). $60.00 – 75.00.

78. CHILDREN'S CHINA, serving pieces from a child's set, traditional *Willow* pattern in dark blue, Ridgways, circa after 1927. Gravy boat and underplate, $100.00 – 120.00; platter, $80.00 – 100.00; covered vegetable dish and underplate, $180.00 – 250.00; dinner plate, $40.00 – 50.00.

79. CHILDREN'S CHINA, mug decorated with a copper lustre finish and a wide blue enameled band, unmarked, circa mid-1800s. $60.00 – 75.00.

80. CHILDREN'S CHINA, waste bowl to a child's tea set, Flow Blue and copper lustre hand-painted *Wheel* pattern, unmarked, circa early to mid 1800s. $100.00 – 125.00.

81. CHILDREN'S CHINA, cup and saucer matching the waste bowl in the preceding picture. $125.00 – 150.00.

82. CHILDREN'S CHINA, plate from a series entitled, "May," brown transfer with a lustre border, ambiguously marked, possibly attributed to Allerton. Registry marks for the following two plates are for the 1880s. $125.00 – 150.00.

83. CHILDREN'S CHINA, "May with Pets," Registry Mark for 1884. $125.00 – 150.00.

84. CHILDREN'S CHINA, "May with Dog," Registry Mark for 1887. $125.00 – 150.00.

Chocolate Pot, a pot similar to a coffee pot, but made with a short spout, for serving hot chocolate. Individual chocolate cups were usually made in the same pattern to form a set. English manufacturers seem to have produced fewer of these than other European china companies.

85. CHOCOLATE POT, Flow Blue *Watteau* scenic pattern, Royal Doulton, circa 1930s. $250.00 – 350.00.

86. CHOCOLATE POT, *Two Temples II Willow* pattern, matching cups. The pot is unmarked, but the cups are marked, "Hammersley's China England," an unidentified company, and "Pitkin & Brooks, Chicago" (retailer), circa early 1900s. Chocolate pot, $225.00 – 275.00; cups, $50.00 – 65.00 each.

Chowder Cup, an oversize cup for serving chowder or mush, usually made with a matching saucer. Also see Mush Cup.

87. CHOWDER CUPS, *Bible* polychrome pattern in orange, yellow-gold, blue, and green on a cream colored body, Ashworth, after 1891. $150.00 – 175.00 each set.

Clock, ceramic cases for clocks were made by many china factories. Sometimes matching vases were made to form a mantel set. Also see Mantel Set.

88. CLOCK, traditional *Willow* pattern on a deeply ruffled dish fitted with a clock face in a brass frame, Doulton, circa 1882 – 1890. The clock was made by British United Clock Co. $600.00 – 700.00.

Coaster, small flat rimmed plates to hold cups or glasses to protect table tops. The one shown is encased in an oak and metal surround, but most were not. Examples are also found printed with advertising and were used in pubs and restaurants.

89. COASTER, traditional *Willow* pattern, George Jones & Sons, circa 1920s – 1940s. $60.00 – 70.00.

Coffee Can, a small, straight-sided cup for serving coffee.

90. **Coffee Cans,** porcelain, gilded décor, Worcester, circa 1790. $175.00 – 200.00 each.

91. **Coffee Cans,** porcelain, Imari colors of cobalt blue and burnt-orange decorate the flower and leaf designs, attributed to New Hall Porcelain Works, circa early 1800s. $225.00 – 250.00 each.

92. **Coffee Can,** porcelain, *Two Temples II Willow* pattern with gilded trim, attributed to New Hall Porcelain Works, circa 1795. $250.00 – 275.00.

93. COFFEE POT, *Chelsea Grape* pattern with copper lustre on a white ironstone body, unmarked, but attributed to Edward Walley, circa 1845 – 1856. $200.00 – 250.00.

Coffee Pot, taller than a teapot, it also has a longer spout than found on a chocolate pot. Many examples have fancy handles.

94. COFFEE POT, Flow Blue Oriental scenic pattern, *Whampoa*, Mellor, Venables & Co., circa 1830s. $1,400.00 – 1,600.00.

95. COFFEE POT, dark blue transfer pattern featuring a river scene with buildings and mountains in the background, unmarked, circa early 1800s. $1,000.00 – 1,200.00.

96. COFFEE POT, borders and handle decorated in a dark to light cobalt blue, J. & G. Meakin, 1890 – 1912. $500.00 – 600.00.

97. COFFEE POT, *Old Castle* pattern in a brown floral transfer with cobalt blue leaves, Enoch Wedgwood, circa 1965. $175.00 – 225.00.

Coffee Urn, a large dispenser for coffee, called an urn because of its shape and lid, like a funeral urn.

98. COFFEE URN, with revolving tray, *Two Temples II Willow* pattern decorates the tray, and *Two Temples I Willow* pattern covers the urn, W. T. Copeland, Godden Mark 1073, impressed mark for 1883. $3,000.00 – 4,000.00.

Comb Holder, a wall pocket vase, for holding combs.

99. COMB HOLDER, traditional *Willow* pattern in red with gold trim, unmarked, except for a Registry Number for the late 1800s. $125.00 – 175.00.

Compote, a coup-shaped bowl on a footed pedestal base.

100. COMPOTE, majolica, large green leaf décor with yellow trim, George Jones, circa 1861 – 1873. $1,200.00 – 1,400.00.

101. COMPOTE, Mason's Oriental scenic pattern, *Chinese Mountain,* in polychrome colors dominated by a burnt-orange. A tea house and a small mountain form the primary design, Charles James Mason & Co., circa 1830 – 1835. $800.00 – 1,000.00.

102. COMPOTE, *Mandarin Willow* pattern in light blue, W. T. Copeland, late 1800s. $225.00 – 275.00.

103. COMPOTE, Flow Blue polychrome *Nankin Jar* floral pattern with gold accents, Doulton, circa early 1900s. $1,000.00 – 1,200.00.

104. COMPOTE, polychrome floral pattern in slate blue and burnt orange, *Paxton*, Francis Morley & Co., circa 1845 – 1858. $400.00 – 500.00.

105. COMPOTE, cobalt blue floral pattern with gold sponged accents, unmarked, circa early 1900s. $125.00 – 145.00.

Condiment Set, a holder or small tray, made of metal or ceramic, containing a dish for salt, a pepper pot or shaker, and a dish for mustard, all in the same pattern. Also see Mustard Pot, Pepper Pot, and Prestopan.

106. CONDIMENT SET, metal holder with an open salt dish, pepper pot, and mustard pot, *Two Temples II Willow* pattern on body with no border pattern, Taylor, Tunnicliff & Co., circa 1875 – 1898. $350.00 – 400.00 set.

107. **CONDIMENT SET,** clover leaf shaped tray with an open salt dish, mustard pot, and pepper shaker, traditional *Willow* pattern, unidentified company, marked "Old Willow Pattern," twentieth century. $250.00 – 275.00 set.

Cow Creamer, a figural creamer in the form of a cow, fitted with a stoppered opening on top to pour in the cream which then could be poured out of the cow's mouth. These were Staffordshire novelty items. Note that they are being reproduced today.

108. **COW CREAMERS,** Jackfield Ware, a red clay body with a glossy black glaze, unmarked, circa 1860. $300.00 – 350.00 each.

109. **COW CREAMER,** traditional *Willow* pattern, unmarked, mid-1800s. $1,400.00 – 1,500.00.

Cream Soup Cup, a two handled cup for serving a cream soup or broth, made with a matching saucer. These sometimes had lids as well.

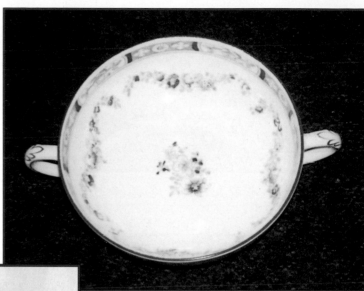

110. CREAM SOUP CUP, multicolored floral garlands decorate cup's interior, Mintons, circa 1891 – 1902. $100.00 – 125.00.

111. CREAM SOUP CUP, with saucer, traditional *Willow* pattern, Ridgways, circa 1927 and after. $75.00 – 100.00.

112. CREAM SOUP CUP, *Canton Willow* pattern, Wood & Sons, Ltd., circa 1917 and after. $30.00 – 40.00.

113. Cream Soup Cup and Saucer, polychrome floral pattern, wine enamel and gold painted borders, Johnson Bros., circa after 1913. $75.00 – 95.00.

114. Cream Soup Cup, with lid and saucer, traditional *Willow* pattern, Josiah Wedgwood, circa after 1891. $225.00 – 275.00 set.

Creamer, a small pitcher, two to three inches high, for serving cream. Also see Sparrow Beak Creamer.

115. Creamer, 3¼"h, pulled strap style handle, Oriental scenic transfer pattern in blue, unmarked, circa 1800. $80.00 – 100.00.

116. CREAMER, 2½"h, Jaspar Ware decorated with classical figures in relief on a blue ground, Josiah Wedgwood, circa 1850. $125.00 – 150.00.

117. CREAMER, 2"h, *Turner Willow* pattern, marked, "Royal Worcester." $75.00 – 85.00.

Crescent Plate, a half-moon shaped plate. Also see Turkey Bone Dish.

118. CRESCENT PLATE, 9¼"l, porcelain, a wide basketweave border surrounds a partial traditional *Willow* pattern, Brown-Westhead, Moore & Co., circa mid- to late 1800s. $125.00 – 150.00.

Cup Plate, a small plate, a little over four inches in diameter, matching a tea cup and saucer, to be used to hold the cup after the tea had been poured out of the cup into the saucer to drink!

119. CUP PLATE, Flow Blue *Coburg* scenic pattern, John Edwards, circa 1847 – 1873. $100.00 – 125.00.

120. CUP PLATE, mulberry transfer of a frolicking dog, unmarked, circa 1840s. $75.00 – 100.00.

121. CUP PLATE, dark brown floral transfer composes a wide border pattern, embellished with a portrait cameo at the top and a monogram, "MMR," William Adams, circa mid-1800s. $60.00 – 80.00.

122. Cup Plate, blue transfer scrolled pattern covers plate, unmarked, circa mid-1800s. $50.00 – 70.00.

Cuspidor, a deep jar with a flared mouth, for expectorating tobacco! These were less grandly called "Spittoons."

123. Cuspidor, traditional *Willow* pattern, Doulton, circa 1891 – 1902. $400.00 – 500.00.

Demi-tasse Cup, a cup smaller than a tea cup, usually made with straight sides, for after-dinner coffee, normally a strong coffee or espresso.

124. Demi-tasse Cup and Saucer, *Lynton* polychrome floral pattern, Ridgways, circa 1900. $45.00 – 55.00.

125. **DEMI-TASSE CUP,** *Ventnor* polychrome floral border pattern, Josiah Wedgwood, circa 1898 – 1915. $55.00 – 65.00.

126. **DEMI-TASSE CUP AND SAUCER,** polychrome floral pattern, Johnson Bros., after 1913. $60.00 – 75.00.

127. **DEMI-TASSE CUP AND SAUCER,** black and orange floral and chain border pattern, William Hudson, Sutherland China, circa 1936. Cup and saucer, $40.00 – 50.00; plate, $30.00 – 35.00.

128. DEMI-TASSE CUP AND SAUCER, Jaspar Ware, classical figural décor in relief on light blue body, Josiah Wedgwood, circa 1891 – 1897. $165.00 – 180.00.

129. DEMI-TASSE CUP AND SAUCER, *Variant Willow* pattern, polychrome with black under-glaze design, Crown Staffordshire Porcelain Company, circa 1906. $60.00 – 75.00.

130. **DEMI-TASSE CUP AND SAUCER,** *Worcester Willow* pattern, Worcester Royal Porcelain Co., Ltd., circa 1884 – 1886. $100.00 – 125.00.

131. **DEMI-TASSE CUP AND SAUCER,** polychrome *Carnival* pattern, an Art Deco design in black and orange, Royal Doulton, circa 1930s. $45.00 – 55.00.

132. **DEMI-TASSE CUP AND SAUCER,** hand-painted red, blue, and green dots on a cream colored background, black trim, Art Deco shape, Sampson Hancock & Sons, circa 1930s. $45.00 – 55.00.

Dessert Stand, a large dish with shallow sides mounted on a short pedestal base, for serving small cakes or various dessert items.

133. DESSERT STAND, 12"l, 3½"h, diamond shaped, *Net* pattern, reserves of pagodas and willow trees on a floral ground form a border on the interior of the dish, Spode, circa 1810. $450.00 – 500.00.

134. DESSERT STAND, floral pattern overlaid in Japan colors over a white ground, "Pearl" impressed mark, attributed to John Ridgway, circa 1830. $400.00 – 450.00.

135. DESSERT STAND, Flow Blue *Sobraon* pattern, Oriental scenic design, unmarked, circa mid-1800s. $500.00 – 600.00.

Dresser Set, matching pieces assembled on a tray for a lady's dressing table, usually including a powder box, trinket box, pin tray, hair receiver, and ring tree. Candle sticks and small vases were also made for some sets.

136. **DRESSER SET,** polychrome Flow Blue floral *Corey Hill* pattern, unmarked except for "England" on back of tray. The pattern is attributed to Ridgways, circa 1880. $800.00 – 1,000.00.

137. **DRESSER SET,** slate blue *Hythe* floral pattern, Keeling & Co., circa 1912 – 1936. $1,000.00 – 1,200.00.

138. DRESSER SET, traditional *Willow* pattern, unmarked, late nineteenth century. $800.00 – 1,000.00.

Egg Coddler, a cup-like dish with a lid designed for cooking an egg by placing the egg in the dish with hot water to cook slowly.

139. EGG CODDLERS, *Worcester Willow* pattern, Worcester Royal Porcelain Company, Ltd., circa 1940s. $100.00 – 125.00 each.

Egg Cup, a small cup with either a flat or pedestal base to hold a boiled egg. Some egg cups are double, meaning that the smaller end can hold the egg in the shell, or the cup can be inverted to the larger end, so that a boiled egg can be unshelled and placed in the cup and not have to be eaten directly from the shell.

140. EGG CUP, single style, reversed *Willow* pattern, Wood & Sons, circa early 1900s. $35.00 – 45.00.

141. Egg Cup, double style, stenciled gold geometric designs and gold bands around borders, marked, Cauldon Ltd., circa 1905 – 1920 and Burley & Co., Chicago, an American importer. $30.00 – 40.00.

Egg Stand, a holder, with or without a handle, made with circular openings to hold boiled eggs.

142. Egg Stand, Flow Blue *Flourette* pattern, Burgess & Leigh, circa early 1900s. $600.00 – 800.00.

143. Egg Stand, Flow Blue *Watteau* scenic pattern, unmarked, circa early 1900s. $400.00 – 600.00.

144. EGG STAND, fitted with a master salt dip on top and pierced slots for egg spoons, traditional *Willow* pattern, unmarked. $800.00 – 1,000.00.

145. EGG STAND, Flow Blue *Wreath* floral pattern, T. Fell & Co., circa mid-1800s. $1,000.00 – 1,200.00.

146. EGG STAND, Flow Blue floral design, unidentified pattern, Wiltshaw & Robinson, circa early 1900s. $300.00 – 400.00.

Ewer, a decorative pitcher with a long slender neck and bulbous body. Originally designed for pouring water, ewers also have a lip.

148. Ewer, Flow Blue *Persian Spray* pattern enhanced with gold, Doulton, circa 1891 – 1902. $500.00 – 600.00.

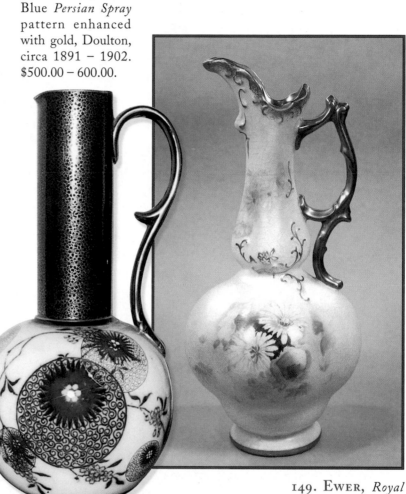

147. Ewer, Flow Blue *Cavendish* floral pattern, Keeling & Co., circa 1912 – 1936. $500.00 – 600.00.

149. Ewer, *Royal Lorne,* multicolored floral pattern, heavy gold trim, S. Fielding & Co., circa 1913. $250.00 – 350.00.

Ferner, a decorative planter.

150. Ferner, Jasper Ware, classical figural décor in relief, Aesculapius and student on a light blue dipped body, Josiah Wedgwood, circa 1890. $500.00 – 600.00.

Fish Platter, a long, narrow platter for serving a whole fish.

151. Fish Platter, Flow Blue *Hong Kong* Oriental scenic pattern, attributed to Charles Meigh, circa 1835 – 1861. $1,200.00 – 1,400.00.

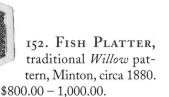

152. Fish Platter, traditional *Willow* pattern, Minton, circa 1880. $800.00 – 1,000.00.

Fish Serving Fork and Knife, similar to a carving set, except in design. The fish knife has a wide non-serrated blade, and the fork is also wide with several tines.

153. Fish Serving Fork & Knife, in original case, electroplated nickel silver with porcelain handles, traditional *Willow* pattern, unmarked, circa late 1800s. $300.00 – 350.00 set.

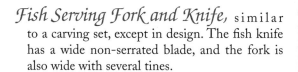

154. Fish Serving Fork & Knife, Jaspar Ware handles decorated with acanthus leaves, made by Josiah Wedgwood, sterling silver hasps on Sheffield plate by Mappin & Webb, circa 1891 – 1897. $350.00 – 450.00 set.

Folded Edge Plate, a square plate with the four corners turned over, sometimes referred to as a "napkin fold" edge.

155. FOLDED EDGE PLATE, *Two Temples II Willow* pattern, gold trim, Sampson Bridgwood & Son, circa 1885. $80.00 – 100.00.

156. FOLDED EDGE PLATE, floral and fruit pattern in dark browns highlighted with blue, Sampson Bridgwood & Son, circa 1885. $60.00 – 75.00.

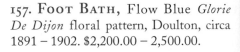

Foot Bath, a large, usually rectangular, bowl for bathing feet, often part of a wash set made in the same pattern.

157. FOOT BATH, Flow Blue *Glorie De Dijon* floral pattern, Doulton, circa 1891 – 1902. $2,200.00 – 2,500.00.

158. Foot Bath, 17"l x 14½"w, unidentified blue floral transfer pattern, unmarked, circa early 1900s. $2,000.00 – 2,200.00.

Ginger Jar, a container with a round or ovoid shaped body, fitted with a lid.

Game Plate, a plate decorated with wild game birds or other wild life such as rabbits or deer, often part of a set consisting of a large serving platter and several, six to twelve, individual plates decorated with different game or game birds. Also see Turkey Plate.

159. Ginger Jar, *Turner Willow* pattern in pink, G. L. Ashworth, circa after 1891. $120.00 – 140.00.

160. Game Bird Plate, Goose and Gander center décor with reserves of cherubs and animals around border, transfer design overlaid with hand-painted work. Josiah Wedgwood, circa 1891 – 1909. $150.00 – 185.00.

Grill Plate, a divided plate designed for restaurant use. The plate had three sections, a large one for meat, and two smaller ones for vegetables.

161. GRILL PLATE, *Booths Willow* pattern, circa early 1900s. $50.00 – 60.00.

Handleless Cup, a cup with straight or paneled sides and no handle. Also see Tea Bowl.

162. HANDLELESS CUP with saucer and cup plate (see Cup Plates), *Athens* transfer scenic pattern in Flow Blue, W. Adams & Sons, circa 1849. $200.00 – 225.00.

163. HANDLELESS CUP with saucer, *Cleopatra* pattern, mulberry transfer with some hand-colored work, marked with pattern name only, circa early to mid-1800s. $100.00 – 125.00.

164. HANDLELESS CUP with saucer, Flow Blue *Jeddo* Oriental scenic pattern, W. Adams & Sons, circa mid-1800s. $225.00 – 250.00.

165. HANDLELESS CUP with saucer, Flow Blue *Manilla* Oriental scenic pattern, Podmore, Walker & Co., circa 1834 – 1859. $250.00 – 275.00.

166. HANDLELESS CUP and saucer, polychrome fruit and floral transfer, unmarked, circa mid-1800s. $100.00 – 125.00.

167. HANDLELESS CUP, black scenic transfer of a house and a lake, unmarked, circa early to mid-1800s. $75.00 – 100.00.

168. HANDLELESS CUP and saucer, enameled fruit and leaves with pink lustre trim, unmarked, circa early to mid-1800s. $100.00 – 125.00.

169. HANDLELESS CUP and saucer, *Tulip* hand-painted Flow Blue pattern enhanced with lustre bands, attributed to Elsmore & Forster (see Williams II, p. 222 and Williams III, p. 64), circa 1860s. $175.00 – 200.00.

170. HANDLELESS CUP and saucer, polychrome Flow Blue floral pattern, unmarked, circa early to mid-1800s. $100.00 – 125.00.

171. HANDLELESS CUPS, Gaudy Flow Blue: left, *Grape* pattern with copper lustre; center, *Wild Rose* pattern; right, unidentified floral pattern; unmarked, circa early 1800s. $100.00 – 125.00 each.

Horseradish Dish, a deep cup-like dish for serving horseradish or other condiments.

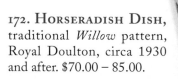

172. HORSERADISH DISH, traditional *Willow* pattern, Royal Doulton, circa 1930 and after. $70.00 – 85.00.

Hot Water Jug, a pitcher for hot water fitted with a small bowl to hold hot water to keep the water warm in the pitcher. Such jugs were part of wash sets but relatively few examples are found.

173. Hot Water Jug, and under bowl, with a perforated liner which sits on under bowl to hold a sponge, Flow Blue *Petunia* floral pattern, H. Bros., unidentified manufacturer. $500.00 – 600.00.

Hot Water Plate, also called a "warming plate," made with a deep base and opening into which hot water is poured to keep the food in the serving dish warm. Usually such dishes are made entirely of china, but sometimes the base may be made of metal, such as copper.

174. Hot Water Dish, oval shape, Flow Blue *Madras* scenic pattern, Royal Doulton, circa 1930s. $600.00 – 700.00.

175. Hot Water Plate, with metal base, unmarked, unidentified slate blue pattern featuring a pitcher type vase on the right and a large floral design on the left, circa late 1800s. $250.00 – 300.00.

176. Hot Water Plate, unidentified blue and white Oriental scenic pattern with a butterfly border, but not actually a willow pattern, unmarked, circa mid- to late 1800s. $400.00 – 500.00.

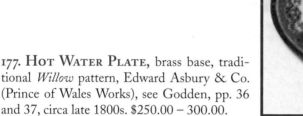

177. Hot Water Plate, brass base, traditional *Willow* pattern, Edward Asbury & Co. (Prince of Wales Works), see Godden, pp. 36 and 37, circa late 1800s. $250.00 – 300.00.

Hotel Ware, heavy crockery or stoneware, thick and durable ceramics, as compared to bone china or semi-porcelain, used in restaurants or hotels. Examples are often marked with the name of a restaurant or hotel, or have "Hotel Ware" as part of the mark.

178. Hotel Ware, traditional *Willow* pattern in blue, marked "Willow, Grindley, England, Hotel Ware," circa 1930s. Serving platter, $40.00 – 60.00; vegetable bowl, $25.00 – 35.00; demi-tasse cup and saucer, $25.00 – 30.00; tea cup and saucer, $25.00 – 30.00.

Humidor, a covered container for storing pipe tobacco or cigars. Humidors were designed to keep the contents fresh by a device, usually under the lid, to hold a piece of apple or sponge to emit moisture.

180. HUMIDOR, traditional *Willow* pattern in brown, Doulton, circa 1890s. $325.00 – 375.00.

179. HUMIDOR, *Worcester Variant Willow* pattern in Flow Blue, Wiltshaw & Robinson, see Godden Mark 4201, circa 1900. $400.00 – 500.00.

Hunt Jug, a pitcher distinguished by relief designs depicting hunting dogs or hunting scenes.

181. HUNT JUG, ironstone, hunting dogs in high relief, accented by intricate scenic designs. Charles James Mason, circa 1845 – 1848. In addition to the Mason mark, an applied pad mark, impressed with "TOHO," a command for a hunting dog "to stop," is on the base of this piece. $1,200.00 – 1,400.00.

Ice Cup, a small cup with a short foot or pedestal base, for serving ices such as sorbet or ice cream. Also see Punch Cup.

182. Ice Cup, porcelain, green enamel and gilt, unmarked, attributed to Worcester, Flight Barr & Barr period, circa 1813 – 1840. $175.00 – 200.00.

183. Ice Cup, white ceramic body decorated with a sprig floral design in cobalt blue, unmarked, circa mid-1800s. $100.00 – 125.00.

Inkwell, small ceramic pots for holding ink, often fitted in a holder or accompanied by a matching tray or stand.

184. Inkwells, double style, traditional *Willow* pattern, Booths, circa early 1900s. $550.00 – 650.00.

185. Inkwells, Jaspar Ware, two pots (lids missing), on an ink stand, classical figures, the "Three Graces" and various Cupid scenes form relief decoration on the cobalt blue dipped body, Josiah Wedgwood, circa 1760 – 1780. $1,000.00 – 1,200.00.

Invalid Feeder, a bowl with a long spout, serving as a straw, so that liquid in the dish can be easily sipped, with a half cover over the top.

Jam Pot, covered jar for jellies or jams.

186. INVALID FEEDER, bowl shaped with half cover, unidentified Flow Blue floral pattern, unidentified monogram mark "TW" with London, very similar to Godden Mark 3885 for William Tudor, circa 1947. $225.00 – 275.00.

187. JAM POT, hinged metal lid, Flow Blue *Percy* scenic pattern, attributed to Francis Morley, circa mid-1800s, see Williams III, p. 18. $175.00 – 225.00.

188. JAM POT, *Canton Willow* pattern, Copeland, circa 1875 – 1890. $200.00 – 225.00.

189. JAM POTS, two covered pots in a handled holder, Gaudy Welsh decoration, Wade & Co., circa 1887 – 1927. $250.00 – 275.00 set.

Jam Dish, a small side dish for individual servings of jam, jelly, or honey.

190. JAM DISH, individual size, restaurant ware, traditional *Willow* pattern, Wood & Sons, circa 1971. $12.00 – 15.00.

Jardiniere, a decorative, deep ceramic pot made for planting flower bulbs, seeds, holding a mature plant, or holding a plant already potted. Often, a matching stand accompanies the piece.

191. JARDINIERE, *Etna* floral pattern, Crown Devon Ware by S. Fielding & Co., circa 1913. $175.00 – 225.00.

192. JARDINIERE, Flow Blue *Rose* floral pattern, Myott, Son & Co., circa early 1900s. $600.00 – 700.00.

193. **JARDINIERE,** footed base, unidentified Flow Blue floral pattern, Thomas Forester & Sons, circa 1891 – 1912. $500.00 – 600.00.

194. **JARDINIERE,** traditional *Willow* pattern, John Tams Ltd. (Tams Ware), circa after 1930. $300.00 – 350.00.

195. **JARDINIERE,** Flow Blue traditional *Willow* pattern, Minton, see Godden Marks 2713 and 2714, circa 1900. $600.00 – 700.00.

Jelly Mold, a stoneware mold with impressed decorative patterns for molding gelatin based foods such as salads or desserts.

196. **JELLY MOLD,** deeply impressed geometric designs, unmarked, circa early to mid-1800s. $75.00 – 100.00.

197. JELLY MOLD, impressed swirl or fluted design, unmarked, circa early to mid-1800s. $100.00 – 125.00.

198. JELLY MOLD, round shape, impressed fluted design with a flower in the center, unmarked, circa early to mid-1800s. $100.00 – 125.00.

199. JELLY MOLD, impressed asparagus design in center, unmarked, circa mid- to late 1800s. $100.00 – 125.00.

200. JELLY MOLD, brown lining with deeply fluted design, Moira Pottery Co., Ltd., circa 1922. $75.00 – 100.00.

Knife Rest, a narrow ceramic stand, two to four inches in length, for placing a knife after use. The smaller ones were made for individual place settings, and the larger ones were for a carving knife used at the table.

201. KNIFE REST, 4"l, traditional *Willow* border pattern, unmarked, circa late 1800s. $125.00 – 150.00.

Leaf Dish, a ceramic dish made either in the form of a single natural leaf or incorporating multiple leaves. Small dishes were popular for nuts or pickles Larger ones were often decorative.

Ladle, a dipper with a rounded bowl and long handle for serving soups and sauces. These usually accompany a soup or sauce tureen. Ladles for sauce tureens have shorter handles and smaller bowls than those for soup tureens. Also see Sauce Tureen and Soup Tureen.

202. LADLE for soup tureen, Flow Blue floral *Mona* pattern, Minton & Boyle, circa 1836 – 1841. $250.00 – 300.00.

203. LEAF DISH, majolica, heavily veined, polychrome finish in brown, yellow, and green, unmarked, circa early 1900s. $150.00 – 175.00.

204. Leaf Dishes, traditional *Willow* pattern, unmarked, mid- to late 1800s. Left, $150.00 – 175.00; right, $175.00 – 200.00.

Loving Cup, a cup with two or three handles, often vase shaped, designed for sipping and to pass from one person to another for celebratory purposes. Large ones are often decorated to commemorate some event.

205. Loving Cup, three handles, slate blue floral pattern, Empire Porcelain Company, circa 1940s. $150.00 – 175.00.

206. Loving Cup, two handles, Coronation commemorative decorated with portraits of King George V and Queen Mary, inscribed, "Coronation 1911" and "Ascension 1910," Copeland mark with "T. Goode & Co.," retailer's mark. $1,500.00 – 2,000.00.

Mantel Set, a decoration for the fireplace mantel consisting of a clock, flanked by a pair of vases.

207. **MANTEL SET,** Flow Blue *Venice* scenic pattern, Bishop & Stonier, circa 1891 – 1910. $4,000.00 – 5,000.00.

Master Salt Dish, a small footed dish, 2" to 3" in diameter and 1½" to 2" high, placed at the head of the dining table near the host. Individual salt dishes are much smaller, approximately ½" diameter and ¼" high, and are placed by each diner. Also see Condiment Set.

208. **MASTER SALT DISH,** footed, un-marked, circa 1770, enameled flowers in bright colors, accented with gold trim. $300.00 – 350.00.

209. **MASTER SALT DISH,** pedestal foot, traditional *Willow* pattern, unmarked, circa early 1900s. $175.00 – 200.00.

Match Box, a small ceramic box with lid for holding matches.

210. MATCH BOX, 4⅜"l, with striker under the lid, Jaspar Ware, classical figure in relief on a cobalt blue dipped ground, Josiah Wedgwood, circa 1790 – 1820. $250.00 – 300.00.

Meat Drainer, a large flat perforated insert to fit inside a platter so that juices could drain from the cooked meat.

211. MEAT DRAINER, 13¾"l, *Indian Grasshopper* pattern enameled in bright blue, pale rose, and green. A "grasshopper" can be seen at the center right of the design; Charles James Mason, circa mid-1800s. $300.00 – 350.00.

212. Meat Drainer, 14"l, *Turner Willow* center pattern, unmarked, circa early to mid-1800s. $400.00 – 500.00.

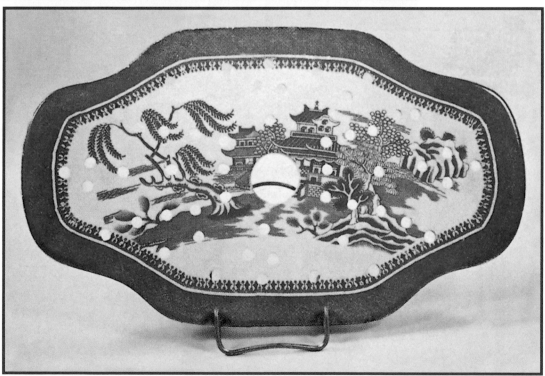

213. Meat Drainer, 16"l, *Canton Willow* pattern, unmarked, circa late 1800s to early 1900s. $350.00 – 400.00.

Milk Jug, a short pitcher, three to six inches high, usually made with a round body and short spout. Although designed for basic utilitarian use, examples are found with a wide range of decorations on different types of ceramic bodies.

214. MILK JUG, 5"h, unmarked, circa 1880, copper lustre finish on body. $125.00 − 140.00.

215. MILK JUG, 5½"h, light blue Jaspar Ware body decorated with classical figures, Josiah Wedgwood, circa 1891 − 1897. $300.00 − 325.00.

216. MILK JUG, 5½"h, *Kyber* polychrome Flow Blue Oriental scenic pattern, W. Adams & Co., circa mid-1800s. $175.00 − 200.00.

217. MILK JUG, 4¼"h, earthenware body decorated with a simple abstract scrolled design, highlighted with gold trim, John Edwards (see Godden Mark 1452), circa 1880 – 1900. $35.00 – 45.00.

218. MILK JUG, earthenware body, figural transfer décor, with hand-painted accents, lustre leaf designs decorate upper border, Gray's Pottery, circa 1933. $100.00 – 125.00.

219. MILK JUG, earthenware body, brown transfer scenic pattern, *Rural England,* W. R. Midwinter, circa 1930s. $80.00 – 100.00.

220. MILK JUG, 4"h, terra cotta (red clay) body painted a bright blue, inscribed with, "The Blue of Devon, Torquay." This jug is an example of "Motto Ware," china decorated with inscriptions, often in the form of old sayings, made by potteries in Torquay in the region of South Devon from the late 1800s. $60.00 – 70.00.

221. MILK JUG, 5"h, earthenware, Chintz multicolored floral pattern, *Marguerite*, Grimwades Royal Winton line, circa 1930s – 1940s. $225.00 – 250.00.

222. MILK JUG, 3½"h, Cream Ware, silver lustre scroll and floral décor, Josiah Wedgwood, circa 1940. $150.00 – 175.00.

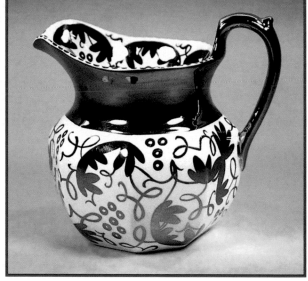

223. MILK JUG, decorated similarly to the preceding piece but on a different body shape, Josiah Wedgwood, circa 1940. $175.00 – 200.00.

Milk Pitcher, a large pitcher distinguished by a metal lid.

224. Milk Pitchers, set of three pitchers with hinged metal lids, *Blue Bell* Flow Blue pattern, unmarked, circa mid-1800s. Left, $600.00 – 800.00; middle, $1,000.00 – 1,200.00; right, $800.00 – 1,000.00.

226. Milk Pitcher, 8"h, hinged metal lid, brown tapestry finish accented with enameled white flowers and green leaves, Doulton (Doulton & Slater's Patent mark), circa 1886 – 1914, with artist's initials, "F.g." $200.00 – 250.00.

225. Milk Pitcher, 7½"h, hinged pewter lid, polychrome floral and leaf pattern, unmarked, circa mid-1800s. $600.00 – 700.00.

227. MILK PITCHER, 7"h, pewter lid, polychrome Flow Blue floral pattern, Samuel Johnson Ltd., circa 1913 – 1931. $175.00 – 225.00.

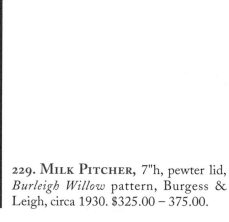

228. MILK PITCHER, 7½"h, pewter lid, Gaudy traditional *Willow* pattern, Gater Hall & Co., circa 1914 – 1943. $225.00 – 275.00.

229. MILK PITCHER, 7"h, pewter lid, *Burleigh Willow* pattern, Burgess & Leigh, circa 1930. $325.00 – 375.00.

Miniature, a small replica of a full-sized object. Ceramic miniatures can be found as salesmen's samples, toy china, or souvenir items. Ceramic miniatures are usually about one-fourth the size of the item they replicate.

230. MINIATURES, Josiah Wedgwood's Jaspar Ware with light blue dipped finish, circa 1891 – 1897: Etruscan jug, 3½"h, classical figures; two handled cup, 1⅜"h, Nike Warriors and classical figures; Brewster flower pot, 2¾"h, classical figures in a Sacrifice scene; vase, 2¾"h, City of London crest. $125.00 – 175.00 each.

231. MINIATURES, Josiah Wedgwood's Jaspar Ware with a cobalt blue finish: pitcher, 2"h, decorated with the Arms of the City of Chester; vase, 2"h, classical brackets with figures of a Nike Warrior, Muses attending Pegasus, and classical figures; loving cup, 1¾"h, figural décor of "Poor Maria" and a boy shepherd, with a crest for Colwyn Bay. $125.00 – 175.00 each.

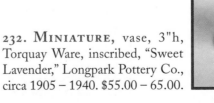

232. MINIATURE, vase, 3"h, Torquay Ware, inscribed, "Sweet Lavender," Longpark Pottery Co., circa 1905 – 1940. $55.00 – 65.00.

233. MINIATURES, pair of vases, 4¾"h, hand-painted sailboats on water, inscribed, "From Ilfracombe," Watcomb Pottery Co., circa 1867 – 1875. $75.00 – 100.00 each.

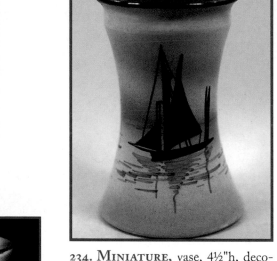

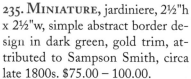

235. MINIATURE, jardiniere, 2½"h x 2½"w, simple abstract border design in dark green, gold trim, attributed to Sampson Smith, circa late 1800s. $75.00 – 100.00.

234. MINIATURE, vase, 4½"h, decorated similarly to the preceding examples, Watcomb Pottery Co., circa 1867 – 1875. $100.00 – 120.00.

Mitten Relish Dish, an elongated dish with one end rounded, like a mitten, and the other end designed as a handle.

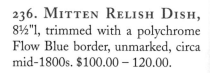

236. MITTEN RELISH DISH, 8½"l, trimmed with a polychrome Flow Blue border, unmarked, circa mid-1800s. $100.00 – 120.00.

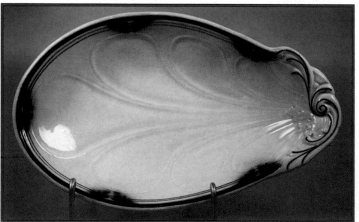

237. MITTEN RELISH DISH, mulberry transfer, *Pelew* scenic Oriental pattern, E. Challinor, circa 1842 – 1867. $120.00 – 140.00.

238. MITTEN RELISH DISH, brown transfer, *Peray* floral pattern. The mark on this piece is the same as one used by Thomas Rathbone, circa 1912, but the mark has the initials, "J. B." instead of "T. R. & Co." $100.00 – 120.00.

239. MITTEN RELISH DISH, 9½"l, traditional *Willow* pattern, W. Adams & Co., circa 1893 – 1917, see Godden Mark 27. $135.00 – 150.00.

Mixing Bowl, a large deep bowl for mixing batters for cakes or dough.

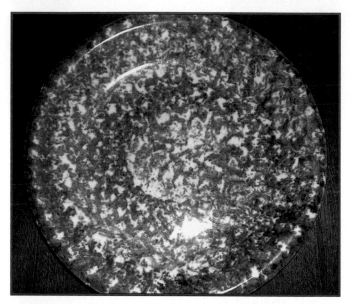

240. MIXING BOWL, sponged décor in deep blue on white earthenware, unmarked, circa late 1800s. $150.00 – 200.00.

Muffin Dish, a deep bowl with a pierced lid, to allow steam to excape from baked goods such as muffins or pancakes, to avoid sweating.

242. MUFFIN DISH, traditional *Willow* pattern, illegible mark, circa early 1900s. $200.00 – 250.00.

Mortar & Pestle, a set consisting of a deep dish, usually made of stoneware, with a stick-shaped instrument, also made of stoneware, or combined with wood on the upper half. The mortar, or bowl, held herbs or other substances which could be ground into a powder by the stick-shaped pestle. Mortars and pestles were used by cooks, but they were also used by pharmacies for concocting medicines.

241. MORTAR & PESTLE, stoneware, decorated with the mark of Charles James Mason in cobalt blue, circa 1820. $1,800.00 – 2,000.00.

Mug, a cup, often, but not always, made with straight sides. The main difference between a cup and a mug is that a cup was made with a matching saucer.

243. MUG, 2½"h, a magenta Oriental scenic pattern decorates the mug in a reserve outlined with a pink lustre design on a cobalt blue glazed body, unmarked, circa 1820. $150.00 – 175.00.

244. MUG, 4"h, decorated with colored enamels over applied figures and middle section, trimmed with pink lustre borders, unmarked, circa 1840. $140.00 – 165.00.

245. MUG, Cream Ware, pâte sur pâte classical figures are framed with a simple silver lustre floral design, unmarked, circa late 1700s. $150.00 – 175.00.

246. MUG, 4½"h, Flow Blue *Nankin* Oriental floral pattern, unmarked, attributed to Ashworth, circa mid-1860s, see Williams I, p. 194. $200.00 – 250.00.

247. MUG, large size, floral pattern, transfer outline with hand-painted colors, W. Adams & Co. Calynx Ware, circa early 1900s. $125.00 – 150.00.

Mush Cup, an oversize cup, for serving mush or cereal.

248. MUSH CUP, black transfer scene of a hunter with his dogs, Copeland, after 1891. $125.00 – 150.00.

249. MUSH CUP, 3½"h x 5¾"w, *Two Temples II Reversed Willow* pattern in green, unmarked, circa early 1900s. $100.00 – 125.00.

250. MUSH CUP, 4¾"d, mauve transfer pattern of an abbey, marked with the pattern name, *Abbess,* which refers to the mother superior of a convent, Wood & Sons, circa 1930s. $120.00 – 140.00.

Mush Set, a bowl for serving mush or cereal, accompanied with an individual size pitcher for milk or syrup.

251. MUSH SET, multicolored floral pattern, Mintons, circa 1891 – 1902. $100.00 – 120.00 set.

Mustache Cup, a cup made with an interior "shelf" with a slit, or opening, at the edge of the cup, so that a man's mustache could rest on the shelf and thus remain dry while he was sipping!

252. MUSTACHE CUP, traditional *Willow* pattern, gold trim, Mintons, circa 1891 – 1902. $225.00 – 250.00.

Mustard Pot, a small covered dish for serving mustard. A tiny ladle usually accompanies a mustard pot, thus the lid may have an opening on one side to hold the ladle. Mustard pots may be found in sets with salt and pepper shakers. Also see Condiment Sets.

253. MUSTARD POT, 3"h, hinged metal lid, cobalt blue hand-painted work with copper lustre, unmarked, mid- to late 1800s. $200.00 – 250.00.

254. MUSTARD POT, traditional *Willow* pattern, unmarked, circa 1920s – 1930s. $80.00 – 100.00.

255. MUSTARD POT, 3½"h, metal lid, multicolored *Two Temples II Willow Simplified* center pattern, pictorial border, Parrott & Co., circa 1935 and after. $100.00 – 125.00.

North Wind Pitcher, a popular name given to a pitcher having a man's face molded under the spout. The rendition of the face is usually grotesque in design with flowing hair and beard. Such pieces are scarce.

256. NORTH WIND PITCHER, 5½"h, unidentified Flow Blue Oriental floral pattern, unmarked, circa mid-1800s. $600.00 – 700.00.

257. NORTH WIND PITCHER, 6"h, Flow Blue *Grecian Scroll* scenic pattern, T. J. & J. Mayer, circa mid-1800s. $700.00 – 800.00.

One Handled Dish, an irregular shaped bowl with a handle on one end. Small ones may have been used for nuts or pickles and larger ones for fruit.

258. One Handled Dish, 5½"d, scalloped edge, undecorated handle, traditional *Willow* pattern, unmarked, nineteenth century. $100.00 – 120.00.

259. One Handled Dish, 11"l, polychrome *Fruit Basket* pattern, unmarked, except for pattern name, possibly made by William Smith & Co., circa 1845, see Williams, 1978, p. 632. $140.00 – 165.00.

260. One Handled Dish, Spode's *Tower* scenic pattern in blue, circa 1820. $400.00 – 450.00.

Oyster Plate, a special plate made with indentations to hold the oysters.

261. Oyster Plate, deep cobalt blue with gold accents frames the center indentations, Doulton, circa early 1900s. $300.00 – 350.00.

262. Oyster Plate, Flow Blue *Delft* floral pattern, Mintons, circa 1873 – 1891. $250.00 – 300.00.

Pepper Pot, a dish with a perforated lid for dispensing ground pepper. Also see Condiment Set, Sugar Duster, and Prestopans.

263. Pepper Pot, 3"h, perforated metal lid, dark cobalt blue hand-painted work with copper lustre on ceramic body, unmarked, circa late 1800s. $225.00 – 250.00.

Perfume Bottle, a ceramic jar with a stopper. Glass is the most common material for perfume bottles. Also see Dresser Set.

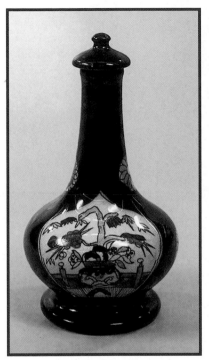

264. PERFUME BOTTLE, 4½"h, a dark cobalt blue finish on body frames a polychrome Oriental floral pattern on a white ground, unmarked, attributed to Charles James Mason & Co., circa 1835. $800.00 – 1,000.00.

265. PERFUME BOTTLE, 6"h, *Mandarin Willow* pattern, Copeland, circa mid to late 1800s. $350.00 – 400.00.

266. PERFUME BOTTLE, 3¾"h x 4¾"sq, unidentified Flow Blue Oriental scenic pattern, accented with gold, unmarked, circa late 1800s. $1,000.00 – 1,200.00.

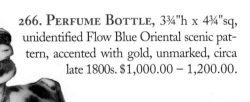

267. PITCHER, ironstone, hand-painted *Sprig* décor in cobalt blue and red, unmarked, circa mid-1800s. $175.00 – 225.00.

Pitcher, a hollow receptacle for holding liquids, which has a handle and a spout. Pitchers were made in all shapes and sizes. Some, because of their size or design, are designated by other names such as cream pitchers, which are small, and water pitchers which are large.

269. PITCHER, 9"h, un-identified floral transfer pattern accented with pink and copper lustre, unmarked, circa mid-1800s. $175.00 – 225.00.

268. PITCHER, 6½"h, Gaudy Dutch style floral décor, Royal Doulton, circa early 1900s.

270. PITCHER, *Peking Japan* Oriental scenic pattern, Charles James Mason, circa 1830. $600.00 – 700.00.

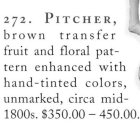

272. PITCHER, brown transfer fruit and floral pattern enhanced with hand-tinted colors, unmarked, circa mid-1800s. $350.00 – 450.00.

271. PITCHER, *Athens* scenic transfer pattern in Flow Blue, W. Adams & Sons, circa 1849. $500.00 – 600.00.

273. PITCHER, Flow Blue *Ferrara* scenic pattern, Josiah Wedgwood, circa early 1900s. $300.00 – 400.00.

274. PITCHER, 6½"h, *Flora* pattern, W. H. Grindley, circa 1890. $100.00 – 125.00.

275. PITCHER, 7"h, gilded scroll work on upper body, W. H. Grindley, circa early 1900s. $60.00 – 75.00.

276. PITCHER, Chintz *Black Pekin* pattern, Grimwades Royal Winton line, circa 1930s – 1940s. $200.00 – 225.00.

277. PITCHER, 7½"h, floral pattern overlaid with copper lustre, Josiah Wedgwood, circa mid-1900s. $175.00 – 200.00.

Plate, a dish with a recessed center and a flanged rim. The rim may be paneled, scalloped, or smooth in shape. For dinnerware, the size of the plate determines its use: bread and butter plate, 5" to 6"; dinner plate, 9" to 10"; salad or dessert plate, 7" to 8"; service plate, 10" to 12"; soup plate, 8" to 9". Dinnerware plates shown here assume dinner size and thus values are listed only for that size plate. English china provides many opportunities for special plate collections. A sample of these is at the end of the plate section. These include armorial or crested decoration and commemorative or souvenir decoration. These plates are valued according to their decoration, age, and rarity.

········ Dinnerware Plates ········

278. PLATE, semi-porcelain, scalloped rim trimmed in gold, deep wine enameled inner border, undecorated center, George Grainger & Co., Worcester, circa 1848. $150.00 – 175.00.

279. PLATE, Jaspar Ware, smooth rim, oak leaf and acorn with acanthus leaves relief décor, Josiah Wedgwood, circa 1891 – 1896. $100.00 – 125.00.

280. PLATE, paneled rim, blue and white transfer floral border with a brown transfer of a rural scenic pattern accented with blue, A. J. Wilkinson, Royal Staffordshire Pottery, circa 1907. $70.00 – $85.00.

281. **PLATE,** scalloped border, multicolored floral pattern decorates center with well and rim of plate trimmed in blue, Copeland, circa 1919. $30.00 – 40.00.

282. **PLATE,** smooth rim, unidentified brown transfer floral pattern, Thomas Elsmore & Son, circa 1878. $60.00 – 75.00 (mc).

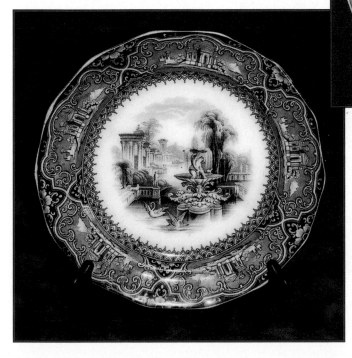

283. **PLATE,** paneled rim, Flow Blue scenic pattern, *Athens*, W. Adams & Sons, circa 1849. $120.00 – 140.00.

284. PLATE, smooth rim, brown floral transfer pattern, *Beatrice*, Wedgwood & Co., circa 1880. $70.00 – 85.00.

285. PLATE, smooth rim, *Canton Willow* pattern, Ashworth Bros., circa early 1900s. $35.00 – 45.00.

286. PLATE, paneled rim, red transfer floral pattern, *Cleopatra*, with hand-tinted accents in blue and green, marked only with pattern name, circa mid-1800s. $100.00 – 125.00.

287. PLATE, scalloped rim, multicolored floral pattern, *Spode's Cowslip*, Copeland, circa mid-1900s. $60.00 – 75.00.

288. **PLATE**, scalloped rim, green floral border pattern, *Derwent*, W. H. Grindley, circa 1891 – 1914. $35.00 – 45.00.

289. **PLATE**, scalloped rim, brown floral border pattern, *Exeter*, F. Winkle & Co., circa 1890 – 1925. $30.00 – 40.00.

290. **PLATE**, smooth rim, *English Scenery*, Wood & Sons, circa 1960. $40.00 – 50.00.

291. **PLATE**, smooth rim, black scenic transfer pattern, *Engrisaille*, marked with a coat of arms and "Birmingham," with a Registry Date of 1869. $75.00 – 100.00.

292. PLATE, smooth rim, *Fallow Deer* scenic pattern, Josiah Wedgwood, circa after 1891. $125.00 – 150.00.

293. PLATE, smooth rim, brown floral pattern, *Hampden*, unmarked, except for pattern name, circa mid- to late 1800s. $40.00 – 50.00 (mc).

294. PLATE, multicolored *Indian Tree* floral pattern, Myott, Son & Co., circa 1930s. $45.00 – 55.00.

295. PLATE, *Landscape* pattern by W. R. Midwinter, circa 1910. $100.00 – 125.00.

296. PLATE, scalloped rim, *Laurier* floral and scroll pattern, Adderleys Ltd., circa 1906 – 1926. $45.00 – 55.00.

297. PLATE, paneled rim, blue scenic pattern, *Lochs of Scotland*, Royal Warwick, unidentified mark, circa mid-1900s. $35.00 – 45.00.

298. PLATE, smooth rim, brown scenic pattern, *Melbourne*, with hand-tinted highlights of medium blue, aqua, and gold, Gildea & Walker, circa 1881. $100.00 – 125.00.

299. PLATE, smooth rim, brown transfer floral pattern, *Morocco*, Thomas Furnival & Sons, circa 1871 – 1890. $50.00 – 60.00.

300. PLATE, scalloped rim, Flow Blue *Ormonde* floral pattern, Alfred Meakin, circa late 1800s. $60.00 – 75.00.

301. PLATE, smooth rim, slate blue *Oxford* floral pattern, W. H. Grindley & Co., circa 1891 – 1914. $50.00 – 65.00.

302. PLATE, smooth rim, blue floral pattern, *Stella*, Bovey Pottery Co., circa early 1900s. $40.00 – 50.00.

303. PLATE, scalloped rim, floral and bird pattern, *The Tigress*, Josiah Wedgwood, circa 1922. $60.00 – 75.00.

304. PLATE, smooth rim, green floral and bird transfer pattern, *Tonquin*, Edge, Malkin & Co., circa 1883. $50.00 – 65.00.

305. **PLATE**, scalloped rim, pink transfer scenic pattern, *Vista*, G. L. Ashworth, circa 1890 – 1900. $60.00 – 75.00.

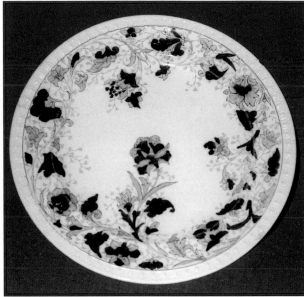

306. **PLATE**, smooth rim, light blue floral pattern highlighted with cobalt blue, Copeland, circa 1847 – 1867. $80.00 – 100.00.

307. **PLATE**, smooth rim, polychrome floral transfer, wine enameled and painted gold borders, Johnson Bros., circa after 1913. $50.00 – 65.00.

COMMEMORATIVE OR SOUVENIR PLATES

308. PLATE, decorated with a crest for the city of Falmouth, England, W. H. Goss, circa late 1800s. $20.00 – 30.00.

309. PLATE, decorated with a shield on a wide lavender border, gold trim, Booths, circa 1912 – 1920. $25.00 – 35.00.

310. PLATE, Abraham Lincoln commemorative, decorated with a figure of Lincoln and five reserves around border depicting Des Moines, Iowa, historical sites, made by Wedgwood & Co., marked, "Expressly for *The Register and Leader Des Moines, Iowa,*" circa early 1900s. $125.00 – 150.00.

311. PLATE, George Washington commemorative in Flow Blue, Royal Doulton, circa 1902 – 1930. $150.00 – 175.00.

312. PLATE, Theodore Roosevelt commemorative in Flow Blue, Rowland & Marcellus importing mark, circa early 1900s. $150.00 – 175.00.

313. PLATE, Alabama State Capitol, Montgomery, souvenir, pink transfer, made by Josiah Wedgwood and marked, "For Klein & Sons Jewelers, Montgomery, Alabama," circa 1911. $60.00 – 75.00.

314. PLATE, Monticello, home of Thomas Jefferson, souvenir, pink transfer, made by Josiah Wedgwood and marked, "Made for the Charlottesville Hardware Company, Charlottesville, Virginia," circa after 1891. $100.00 – 125.00.

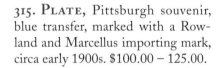

315. PLATE, Pittsburgh souvenir, blue transfer, marked with a Rowland and Marcellus importing mark, circa early 1900s. $100.00 – 125.00.

316. PLATE, marked, "Memorial to George Rogers Clark and The Territories of the American Revolution, The Conquest of the West," pink transfer, made by Josiah Wedgwood for "The Francis Vigo Chapter of The Daughters of the American Revolution," 1931. $100.00 – 125.00.

317. PLATE, Australia souvenir, marked, "Sydney Harbor Bridge, Souvenir Sequi Centenary, 1788 – 1938," polychrome transfer, Royal Doulton. $75.00 – 100.00.

318. PLATE, Canada souvenir, marked, "Canada Coat of Arms," polychrome transfer, Alfred Meakin, circa after 1945. $45.00 – 60.00.

319. PLATE, World War I commemorative, polychrome transfer, flags with a globe, and "Peace, 28th of June, 1919, The Great War," and an eagle and "Victory, 1920," illegible mark. $60.00 – 75.00.

Platter, a large serving dish, oval or rectangular in shape, with a recessed center and flanged rim. The rim may be paneled, scalloped, or smooth. Sizes vary from 9" to 24" in length. Examples shown here are valued for a 14" to 16" size. Note that a complete dinner service usually had several platters in various sizes. Also see Well and Tree Platter.

320. PLATTER, rectangular shape, scalloped rim, unidentified brown floral pattern with hand-tinted color, George Jones & Sons, circa 1884. $175.00 – 225.00.

321. PLATTER, oval shape, scalloped rim, Flow Blue *Ashburton* floral and scroll pattern, W. H. Grindley, circa 1891 – 1914. $250.00 – 300.00.

322. PLATTER, rectangular shape, paneled rim, Flow Blue scenic pattern, *Athens*, W. Adams & Sons, circa 1848. $500.00 – 600.00.

323. PLATTER, rectangular shape, paneled rim, light blue scenic pattern, *Lucerne*, Joseph Clementson, circa 1839 – 1864. $600.00 – 700.00.

324. PLATTER, rectangular shape, scalloped rim, slate blue floral pattern, *Mepsey*, W. H. Grindley, circa 1889. $175.00 – 225.00.

325. PLATTER, rectangular shape, scalloped rim, brown scenic transfer pattern, *Parisian Chateau*, attributed to Ralph Hall, circa 1840s. $600.00 – 700.00.

326. PLATTER, oval shape, scalloped rim, Flow Blue floral pattern, *Richmond*, Burgess & Leigh, circa early 1900s. $225.00 – 275.00.

327. PLATTER, oval shape, smooth rim, slate blue *Strawberry* transfer border pattern, T. G. & F. Booth, circa 1891. $350.00 – 400.00.

328. PLATTER, oval shape, smooth rim, traditional *Willow* pattern, T. W. Barlow & Son Ltd., circa 1928 – 1936. $125.00 – 150.00.

Pocket Watch Holder, a novelty Staffordshire ceramic item, made in various forms, for storing a pocket watch. These might be placed on a mantel or a shelf or a chest.

329. POCKET WATCH HOLDER, made in a fanciful form incorporating a cottage, trees, and cherubs, unmarked, circa early to mid-1800s. $600.00 – 700.00.

Potpourri Dish, a bowl with a pierced cover, designed to hold flowers or petals, allowing their fragrance to escape through the perforated cover. Also see Rose Bowl.

330. POTPOURRI DISH, Jaspar Ware, cobalt finish, Josiah Wedgwood, circa 1840 – 1850. $400.00 – 450.00.

Prestopan, a condiment set in figural form. The name evolved because these items were made by potteries in Prestopan, Scotland, during the early to mid-1800s.

331. PRESTOPANS, figural condiment holders for mustard, pepper, vinegar, and salt. The set is decorated with the traditional *Willow* border pattern on the borders of the hats and bases of the hand-painted figures. Note that the mustard pot has an opening for a small spoon. The pepper holders are shakers, while the vinegar holder has a stopper. The far right figure was designed as an open salt dish rather than a shaker; unmarked, circa early to mid-1800s. $1,800.00 – 2,000.00 set.

Pudding Mold, a deep dish for puddings or desserts.

332. PUDDING MOLD, 4½"h, traditional *Willow* pattern, marked, "England." $80.00 – 100.00.

333. PUDDING MOLD, 3"h, 4½"d, multi-colored *Pagoda* pattern by Davison & Son Ltd, circa 1948 – 1952. This is also called the *Simplified Two Temples II Willow* pattern with a pictorial border. $120.00 – 140.00.

Punch Bowl, a large, deep bowl, with a pedestal, for serving punch. The pedestal may be a separate piece or attached to the bowl.

334. PUNCH BOWL, 9"h, 14½"d, Flow Blue *Vernon* floral pattern, brushed gold accents, Doulton, circa early 1900s. $1,800.00 – 2,200.00.

335. PUNCH BOWL, 6"h, 9"d, traditional *Willow* pattern, Josiah Wedgwood, late 1800s to early 1900s. $1,200.00 – 1,400.00.

Razor Box, a long flat box with cover, for a razor. Some boxes are divided into three sections. Mountfield, p. 201, indicates that the sections are for "other shaving accoutrements;" however, the razor could also rest on top of the sections. Also see Wash Set.

336. Razor Box, Flow Blue floral pattern, *Botanical*, Minton & Co., circa 1841 – 1873. $400.00 – 500.00.

337. Razor Box, with view of interior, brown transfer pattern, *Vesta*, unmarked, except for pattern name, circa mid-1800s. $175.00 – 200.00.

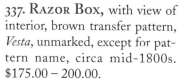

Relish Dish, a dish with sections, sometimes having a center handle, for serving assorted relishes. Also see Mitten Relish Dish.

338. Relish Dish, 11½"d, three sections, Flow Blue unidentified floral pattern, Doulton, circa 1891 – 1902. $300.00 – 350.00.

339. RELISH DISH, 13"d, center handle, *Two Temples II Willow* pattern, unmarked, circa early 1900s. $350.00 – 400.00.

Reticulated Dish, a dish with a perforated edge. Also see Chestnut Bowl.

340. RETICULATED PLATE, Cream Ware, reticulated border with a molded basketweave pattern, Josiah Wedgwood impressed mark with a year cypher for 1861. $175.00 – 200.00.

341. RETICULATED PLATE, Majolica, *Bamboo & Fan* pattern, reticulated outer border, Minton, circa 1875. $150.00 – 175.00.

342. RETICULATED PLATTER,
8¼" x 7¼", reticulated inner
border. *Canton Willow* pattern,
unmarked, circa early 1800s.
$275.00 – 300.00.

Rose Bowl, an open dish for holding
rose petals, allowing their fragrance to
escape. Also see Potpourri Dish.

343. ROSE BOWL, 2¾"h x 3⅝"w, Jaspar Ware, a dark
green glaze covers the parian body, accentuating the
applied relief décor of acorn and leaves, attributed to
Robinson & Ledbeater, marked "R & L, Stoke-on-
Trent," circa before 1891. $150.00 – 200.00.

Salad Set, a large open ceramic
bowl, usually with a metal rim,
accompanied by a fork and spoon
with ceramic handles.

344. SALAD SET, Jaspar Ware, dark
cobalt finish with classical figures in
relief decorates bowl; the handles of
the fork and spoon are decorated with
acanthus leaves, Josiah Wedgwood,
circa 1840. $700.00 – 800.00 set.

345. SALAD SET, Flow Blue *Arundel* floral pattern with brushed gold accents, Doulton, circa 1891 – 1902. $250.00 – 300.00 set.

346. SALAD SET fork and spoon for the preceding picture.

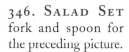

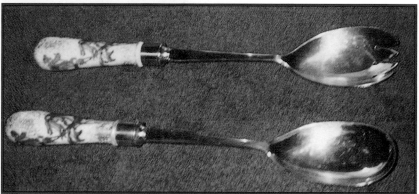

Sauce Boat, an oblong footed dish, with a handle and wide spout, for pouring sauce or gravy.

347. SAUCE BOAT, porcelain, decorated with an enameled *Sprig* pattern in dark blue, pink, and yellow-gold, Derby, circa 1810, see Godden Mark 1253. $275.00 – 300.00.

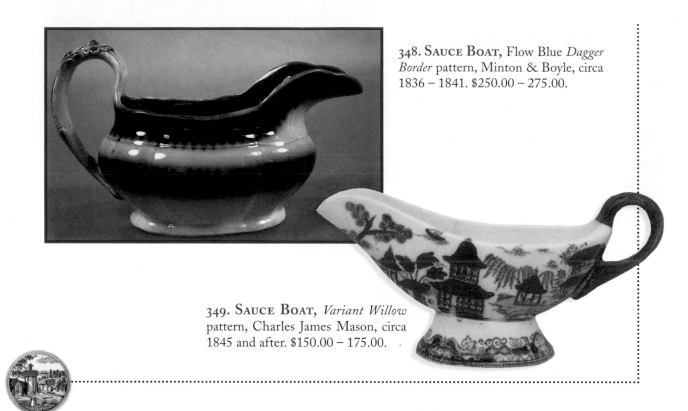

348. Sauce Boat, Flow Blue *Dagger Border* pattern, Minton & Boyle, circa 1836 – 1841. $250.00 – 275.00.

349. Sauce Boat, *Variant Willow* pattern, Charles James Mason, circa 1845 and after. $150.00 – 175.00.

Sauce Tureen, a tureen smaller than a soup tureen, for serving sauces. Sauce tureens usually have a pedestal base, two handles, and an opening in the lid for a ladle. Sauce tureens may have a matching underplate and ladle.

350. Sauce Tureen, Ironstone, *Chusan* Oriental pattern in cobalt blue, burnt orange, and peach over a tinted pale blue ground. The pattern contains the components of a room with urns of flowers and Oriental furniture. William Ridgway & Co., circa 1830 – 1854. $650.00 – 700.00.

351. Sauce Tureen, Oriental landscape pattern with a temple decorates the top of the lid; a diaper design of flowers and geometric shapes forms a wide border on the lid, top of bowl, and the underplate, gold trim, Grainger & Co., circa 1870 – 1889. $275.00 – 325.00.

352. Sauce Tureen, *Kew* floral pattern in blue-green, Furnivals Ltd., circa 1890 – 1895. $250.00 – 300.00.

353. Sauce Tureen, Flow Blue *Princess* pattern, floral garlands and portrait cameos, T. Rathbone, circa 1912 – 1923. $350.00 – 400.00.

354. SAUCE TUREEN, traditional *Willow* pattern, G. Phillips, circa mid-1800s. $350.00 – 375.00.

Scuttle Shaving Mug, a shaving mug made with a holder for the shaving brush. Also see Shaving Mug.

355. SCUTTLE SHAVING MUG, traditional *Willow* pattern, Gibson & Sons Ltd., circa 1912 – 1930. $300.00 – 325.00.

Serving Dish, a large dish, with or without a lid, for serving a variety of foods. Serving dishes differ from vegetable bowls by being larger, having a more elaborate shape, two handles, and often a footed or short pedestal base. Covered serving dishes differ from soup tureens not only in being smaller in size, but they also do not have an opening in the lid for a ladle. Covered dishes are shown first, followed by open examples.

356. SERVING DISH, covered, round shape, pedestal base, unidentified Flow Blue Oriental scenic pattern, Knight Elkin & Co., circa 1826 – 1846, see Godden Mark 2302. $800.00 – 1,000.00.

357. SERVING DISH, covered, 11"d, round shape, Mason's *Rich Ruby* pattern in Japan colors with gold scroll work. The center pattern is an urn filled with multicolored flowers on a white ground. A combination of birds and flowers in light to dark shades of orange on a cobalt blue ground forms the border pattern. Charles James Mason & Co., circa 1829 – 1845. $650.00 – 750.00.

358. SERVING DISH, covered, octagonal shape, pedestal base, Flow Blue *Circassia* scenic pattern, J. & G. Alcock, circa 1839 – 1846. $1,000.00 – 1,200.00.

359. SERVING DISH, covered, rectanglar shape, 12"l, cobalt blue and burnt orange are the primary colors on this bird and floral pattern, unidentified factory, circa 1840 – 1850. $400.00 – 500.00.

360. Serving Dish, covered, octagonal shape, pedestal base, light blue figural scenic transfer, unmarked, circa mid-1800s. $300.00 – 350.00.

361. Serving Dish, covered, octagonal shape, pedestal base, rolled handles, *Athens* scenic pattern in Flow Blue, W. Adams & Sons, circa 1849. $600.00 – 800.00.

362. Serving Dish, covered, round shape, Flow Blue *Blue Bell* pattern, unmarked, circa mid-1800s. $400.00 – 500.00.

363. SERVING DISH
Bowl, rectangular shape, slate blue animal and bird pattern, *Fables*, Brown, Westhead, Moore & Co., circa 1862 – 1884. $400.00 – 500.00.

364. SERVING DISH
Cover for *Fables* pattern.

365. SERVING DISH,
covered, pierced handles, round shape, pedestal base, polychrome floral pattern, W. T. Copeland impressed mark, circa 1847 – 1867. $500.00 – 600.00.

366. Serving Dish, covered, round shape, Flow Blue *Virginia* floral pattern, John Maddock, circa 1880 – 1896. $325.00 – 375.00.

367. Serving Dish, covered, rectangular shape, Flow Blue *Raleigh* floral pattern in an Art Nouveau style, Burgess & Leigh, circa early 1900s. $400.00 – 500.00.

368. Serving Dish, covered, oval shape, slate blue floral pattern, *Iris*, in an Art Nouveau style, A. J. Wilkinson, Royal Staffordshire Pottery, circa 1907, see Godden Mark 4170. $300.00 – 400.00.

369. SERVING DISH, covered, six-sided, Flow Blue *Claremont* floral pattern, Johnson Bros., circa early 1900s. $300.00 – 400.00.

370. SERVING DISH, covered, round shape, Flow Blue *Tokio* floral pattern, Johnson Bros., circa early 1900s. $400.00 – 500.00.

371. SERVING DISH, covered, scalloped footed base, rectangular shape, Flow Blue *Roma* floral pattern, Wedgwood & Co., circa 1900 – 1908. $400.00 – 500.00.

372. SERVING DISH, covered, oval shape, Flow Blue *Granada* floral pattern, Henry Alcock & Co., circa late 1890s. $500.00 – 600.00 (with underplate).

373. SERVING DISH, covered, scalloped pedestal base, oval shape, undecorated except for molded body designs, W. H. Grindley & Co., circa 1914 – 1925. $175.00 – 225.00.

374. SERVING DISH, covered, traditional *Willow* pattern, T. W. Barlow & Son, circa 1930s. $150.00 – 175.00.

375. SERVING DISH, open, divided into four sections, 13"l, 11"w, traditional *Willow* pattern, Spode, circa early 1800s. $1,000.00 – 1,200.00.

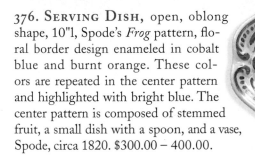

376. SERVING DISH, open, oblong shape, 10"l, Spode's *Frog* pattern, floral border design enameled in cobalt blue and burnt orange. These colors are repeated in the center pattern and highlighted with bright blue. The center pattern is composed of stemmed fruit, a small dish with a spoon, and a vase, Spode, circa 1820. $300.00 – 400.00.

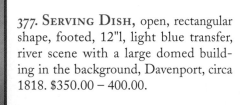

377. SERVING DISH, open, rectangular shape, footed, 12"l, light blue transfer, river scene with a large domed building in the background, Davenport, circa 1818. $350.00 – 400.00.

378. SERVING DISH, open, rectangular shape, 16"l, Mason's *Blue Pheasants* floral and bird pattern in light to dark blue, G. M. & C. J. Mason, circa 1825 – 1829. $600.00 – 700.00.

379. SERVING DISH, open, 9½"l, rectangular shape, Minton's polychrome *Florentine* pattern in orange and gray, Minton & Co., circa 1862. $200.00 – 250.00.

380. SERVING DISH, open, rectangular, 10½"l, light blue transfer, *Asiatic Pheasants*, marked, "K. & Co.," probably Keeling & Co., circa late 1800s. $175.00 – 225.00.

381. SERVING DISH, open, rectangular, 10"l, Johnson Bros., polychrome scenic pattern, *Old British Castle*, in dark green and orange, circa after 1913. $100.00 – 125.00.

382. SERVING DISH, open, 8¼"d, Ashworth's *Decoupage* pattern in black and cobalt blue, circa 1910 and after. $400.00 – 500.00.

383. SERVING DISH, open, footed, 10½"l, Ridgway's *Oriental* figural and scenic pattern in light blue, circa after 1891. $150.00 – 200.00.

Shaving Mug, an oversize cup with straight sides, a handle, and a rim base. Also see Scuttle Shaving Mug and Wash Set.

384. SHAVING MUG, hand-painted Flow Blue and copper lustre pattern, *Wheel,* unmarked, circa mid-1800s. $225.00 – 275.00.

385. SHAVING MUG, Flow Blue polychrome floral pattern with copper lustre, unmarked, circa mid- to late 1800s. $150.00 – 175.00.

Soap Dish, a small dish, usually having a cover, and often a perforated liner to drain the soap. Also see Wash Set.

386. SOAP DISH, Ironstone, undecorated, W. H. Grindley & Co., circa late 1800s. $20.00 – 25.00.

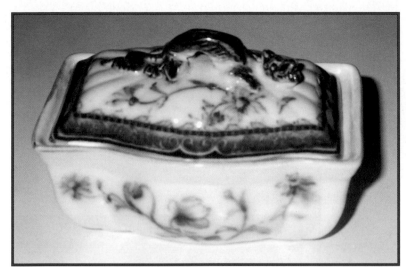

387. SOAP DISH, Flow Blue *Anemone* floral pattern, Bishop & Stonier, circa 1891 – 1910. $250.00 – 275.00.

388. SOAP DISH with liner, traditional *Willow* pattern, Royal Doulton, circa 1930s. $225.00 – 250.00.

389. SOAP DISH, with insert, not shown, ironstone, brown transfer pattern depicting a table with vases, scrolled border designs, unmarked, circa mid- to late 1800s. $50.00 – 65.00.

Soup Bowl, a deep rounded dish, 8" to 9" in diameter, without a flanged rim. Also see Soup Plate.

390. SOUP BOWL, Flow Blue *Florentine* floral pattern, Bourne & Leigh, circa early 1900s. $60.00 – 75.00.

391. SOUP BOWL, Flow Blue *Harvest* floral pattern, see Williams II, p. 138, Alfred Meakin, Ltd., circa early 1900s. $50.00 – 65.00.

392. SOUP BOWL, Flow Blue *Regina* floral pattern, J. & G. Meakin, circa 1912 and after. $70.00 – 85.00.

393. SOUP BOWL, Flow Blue *Yeddo* Oriental scenic pattern, Arthur J. Wilkinson, circa 1907. $100.00 – 125.00.

Soup Plate, a round dish with a flanged rim. Also see Soup Bowl.

394. SOUP PLATE, brown transfer floral pattern, *Balmoral*, with hand-tinted accents, Wood & Hulme, circa 1884. $65.00 – 80.00.

395. SOUP PLATE, polychrome Oriental figural and scenic pattern, *Chang*, Edge, Malkin & Co., circa 1891. $75.00 – 90.00.

396. Soup Plate, brown transfer floral pattern, *Kioto*, Bates, Gildea & Walker, circa 1878 – 1881. $50.00 – 65.00.

397. Soup Plate, brown transfer floral and scenic pattern, *Melbourne*, Gildea & Walker, circa early 1880s. $55.00 – 70.00.

398. Soup Plate, slate blue *Rosaline* floral pattern, Alfred Meakin, circa early 1900s. $45.00 – 60.00.

399. SOUP PLATE, light blue floral transfer pattern, *Stirling*, Keeling & Co. circa 1890. $40.00 – 55.00.

400. SOUP PLATE, brown transfer scenic pattern with inset cameos, *Tennyson*, New Wharf Pottery Co., circa 1884. $60.00 – 75.00.

401. SOUP PLATE, unidentified blue and white Oriental scenic pattern, circa early 1800s. $100.00 – 125.00.

Soup Tureen, a large deep covered dish, usually footed, for serving soups. The lids always have a deep opening for a ladle. Tureen stands or underplates complete the set. Also see Tureen Stand.

402. Soup Tureen, octagonal-shaped pedestal base fits a separate tureen stand, Mulberry *Stick* pattern, an example of "combed" ware, unmarked, circa early to mid 1800s. $1,000.00 – 1,200.00.

403. Soup Tureen, polychrome Flow Blue floral pattern, *Bentick*, Cauldon, circa 1905 – 1920. $800.00 – 1,000.00.

404. Soup Tureen with underplate, Flow Blue *Madras* floral pattern, Doulton, circa early 1900s. $1,600.00 – 1,800.00 set.

405. Soup Tureen with underplate, Flow Blue *Mona* floral pattern, Minton & Boyle, circa 1836 – 1841. $1,800.00 – 2,000.00 set.

406. Soup Tureen with underplate, Flow Blue *Mongolia* scrolled pattern, unmarked, attributed to an unidentified company, F. & W., circa mid- to late 1800s. $1,400.00 – 1,600.00 set.

407. Soup Tureen with underplate, Flow Blue *Venice* pattern, Soho Pottery, circa 1901 – 1906. $600.00 – 800.00.

408. SOUP TUREEN, pink scenic pattern, *Vista*, G. L. Ashworth, after 1891. $1,400.00 – 1,600.00.

409. SOUP TUREEN, traditional *Willow* pattern, unidentified manufacturer, circa late 1800s. $800.00 – 1,000.00.

Sparrow Beak Creamer, a cream pitcher with a sharp pointed spout.

410. SPARROW BEAK CREAMER, enameled *Sprig* floral pattern forms a garland around the interior border and is interspersed with a rather crude dot pattern painted over in a dark pink, unmarked, circa 1780. $250.00 – 275.00.

Spill Holder, a container for holding "spills," which are small pieces of wood or paper used for lighting fires.

411. SPILL HOLDER, made in the form of a castle, 7½"h, unmarked, circa late 1800s. $300.00 – 400.00.

Sponge Holder, a dish with a perforated liner, to hold a bathing sponge. Also see Wash Set.

412. SPONGE HOLDER, 2"h, 8"d, Flow Blue *Bouquet* floral pattern, Furnivals, Ltd., circa after 1913. $225.00 – 275.00.

413. SPONGE HOLDER, Flow Blue *Saskia* floral pattern, Ridgways, circa 1905 – 1920. $225.00 – 275.00.

Stilton Cheese Keeper, a plate with a tall round cover, for storing a round cheese. The name is derived from the cheese-making area of Stilton.

414. STILTON CHEESE KEEPER, 9"h, Jaspar Ware, classical figures and cupids in relief, Josiah Wedgwood, circa 1890. $500.00 – 600.00.

415. STILTON CHEESE KEEPER, Flow Blue *Iris* floral pattern with gold sponged accents, Doulton, circa 1891 – 1902. $800.00 – 1,000.00.

416. STILTON CHEESE KEEPER, Flow Blue *Blossom* floral pattern with gold sponged accents, Sampson Hancock, circa 1906 – 1912. $800.00 – 1,000.00.

Sugar Bowl, a bowl with handles and a lid. Sugar bowls made without covers are called "open" sugars. The size of one's sugar bowl was said to be an indication of wealth when sugar was scarce. Sugar also was sold in cones which required a large container. Sugar bowls made from the early to mid-1800s are large and more massive in appearance than bowls made after that time when granulated sugar became available. Also see Sugar Box.

417. SUGAR BOWL, covered, enameled floral pattern distinguished by large round pink flowers over a cream colored glaze, unmarked, circa 1820. $200.00 – 225.00.

418. SUGAR BOWL, covered, 6"h, soft paste, enameled *Sprig* floral pattern, unmarked, circa early 1800s. $125.00 – 150.00 (mc).

419. SUGAR BOWL, covered, 8"h, ironstone, *Chelsea Grape* pattern, Edward Walley, circa 1845 – 1856, see Godden Mark 3988. $150.00 – 175.00.

420. SUGAR BOWLS, covered, two different shapes, *Athens* Flow Blue scenic pattern, W. Adams & Sons, circa 1849. $500.00 – 700.00 each.

421. SUGAR BOWL, covered, 5½"h, Flow Blue *Coral* floral pattern, Johnson Bros., circa early 1900s. $145.00 – 165.00.

422. SUGAR BOWL, covered, 5½"h, Flow Blue floral pattern, *The Hofburg*, W. H. Grindley & Co., circa 1891 – 1914. $120.00 – 140.00.

423. SUGAR BOWL, covered, 5½"h, traditional *Willow* pattern, Bakewell Bros., circa 1927 – 1943, see Godden Mark 236. $225.00 – 275.00.

424. SUGAR BOWL, open style, 3¾"h, Gaudy Dutch hand-painted floral décor, W. Wood & Co., circa late 1800s. $175.00 – 225.00.

425. SUGAR BOWL, open style, *Booths Willow* pattern, Booths, circa 1912 and after. $80.00 – 100.00.

Sugar Box, a covered sugar bowl without handles.

426. Sugar Box, 4½"h, Jaspar Ware, bright blue body, Josiah Wedgwood, circa 1785. This item is considered rare because it is a Jaspar body without ornamentation. $1,000.00 – 1,200.00.

427. Sugar Box, 3½"h x 5"w, Jaspar Ware, relief cameo portrait of George Washington, Benjamin Franklin is on the reverse, Josiah Wedgwood, circa 1876. $275.00 – 325.00.

Sugar Duster, a tall shaker for dispensing sugar. These may also be called, "muffineers."

428. Sugar Duster, 5"h, figural shape, hand painted, unmarked, circa 1870. $400.00 – 450.00.

429. Sugar Duster, 7"h, multicolored *Reversed Simplified Willow* pattern, metal lid, Lancaster Ltd., circa after 1906. $150.00 – 200.00.

Sweetmeat Tray, individual dishes shaped to fit together to form a whole, for serving an assortment of items. Some were made with lids to cover each section. The dishes may fit inside a tray. "Supper tray" is another term for these dishes.

430. SWEETMEAT TRAY, 13" x 11", porcelain, diamond shaped dishes fit in a six-sided wooden tray, traditional *Willow* pattern, Spode, circa early 1800s. $800.00 – 1,000.00.

431. SWEETMEAT TRAY, 16½"l x 11½"w, seven sections, *Booths Willow* pattern, circa after 1906. $800.00 – 1,000.00.

Syrup Jug, a pitcher, with a metal lid, for pouring syrup. Syrup pitchers are distinguished from milk pitchers, which also have metal lids, being smaller in size, from three to six inches in height.

432. SYRUP JUG, 6"h, *Jackfield* décor, a glossy black glaze covering a terra cotta body, Britannia metal lid, circa early 1800s. $200.00 – 250.00.

433. SYRUP JUG, 5½"h, metal lid, enameled in brown and green with an incised design around center of jug, Gibson & Sons, late 1800s. $50.00 – 65.00.

Tea Bowl, a bowl-shaped cup without handles, usually accompanied by a matching saucer. Tea bowls are often called "handleless cups," but handleless cups have a flared or paneled shape rather than a rounded one. Also see Handleless Cup.

434. TEA BOWL and saucer, enameled floral décor highlighted by a vase of flowers, attributed to the Worcester factory. The molded body design is known as "Worcester Swirl," circa 1800. $225.00 – 275.00.

435. TEA BOWL and saucer, overglaze enameled pink floral pattern with large green leaves, unmarked, circa 1810. $225.00 – 275.00.

436. TEA BOWL and saucer, magenta transfer, *Mount Vernon*, an American view design, silver lustre trim, unmarked, circa 1810. $225.00 – 250.00.

437. TEA BOWL and saucer, porcelain, *Two Temples II Willow* pattern, heavily overlaid with gold scroll work, attributed to New Hall Porcelain Works, circa 1795. $250.00 – 300.00.

Tea Caddy, a jar with a stopper or a lid, for storing tea leaves. A tea caddy is smaller than a tea jar, although the purpose is the same. Also see Tea Jar.

438. TEA CADDY (stopper missing), 5"h, *Variant Willow* pattern in dark blue, gold trim, nineteenth century. $150.00 – 175.00 (with lid).

439. TEA CUP and saucer, pointed handle, soft paste, enameled *Sprig* pattern in magenta and green, unmarked, circa early 1800s. $30.00 – 35.00.

Tea Cup, a one-handled cup with a flared top which is larger than the base. Tea cups are differentiated from coffee cups which have smaller mouths and have a cylinder or paneled shape. For the examples shown, some of the handles are described by terms used by Barber, 1914, pp. 57 – 62. Note that handles were made fancier during the early 1800s than those made later in the century and during the early 1900s.

440. TEA CUP and saucer, pointed handle, enameled pattern featuring a vase and flowers in pink, rust-orange, blue, green, and yellow, unmarked, circa 1820. $100.00 – 125.00.

441. TEA CUP and saucer, pointed handle, black transfer scene of farm animals made by the "bat" transfer method, unmarked, circa early 1800s. $150.00 – 175.00.

442. TEA CUP and saucer, pointed handle, ironstone, *Chelsea Grape* pattern with copper lustre, unmarked, circa 1830. $35.00 – 45.00.

443. TEA CUP and saucer, pointed handle, magenta transfer, bird pattern, unmarked, circa mid-1800s. $100.00 – 120.00.

444. Tea Cup and saucer, slightly pointed shaped handle, ironstone, brown transfer, *Kirkee* Oriental figural and scenic pattern, J. Meir & Son, circa 1890 – 1897. $40.00 – 50.00.

445. Tea Cup and saucer, curved upright handle, pâte sur pâte decoration distinguished by a cherub and a border design of interlocking circles on a lavender ground, Davenport, prior to 1830, see Godden Mark 1191. $275.00 – 300.00.

446. Tea Cup and saucer, rococo handle, enameled magenta transfer figural scene depicting *Charity*, unmarked, circa 1840. $100.00 – 125.00.

447. TEA CUP and saucer, Jaspar Ware, Josiah Wedgwood's "Bute" shape, classical figures and brackets in relief on a blue ground, circa 1850 – 1870. $175.00 – 200.00.

448. TEA CUP and saucer, simple curved handle, black transfer, *Seine* floral pattern, Holmes, Plant & Maydew, circa 1882. $35.00 – 45.00.

449. TEA CUP and saucer, light blue transfer, *Rococo* scroll and floral pattern, John Maddock, circa 1880 – 1896. $30.00 – 40.00.

450. **TEA CUP** and saucer, hand-tinted red transfer floral pattern, unmarked, except with a Registry Number circa 1891. $65.00 – 80.00.

451. **TEA CUP** and saucer, polychrome Oriental floral pattern, G. L. Ashworth, circa 1890s. $50.00 – 65.00.

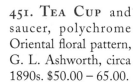

452. **TEA CUP** and saucer, Flow Blue *Arcadia* floral pattern, Arthur J. Wilkinson, circa 1907. $100.00 – 125.00.

453. **Tea Cup,** and saucer, *Bombay* floral transfer pattern in Japan colors highlighted with a heavy application of cobalt blue on the scroll work and floral reserves, John Maddock & Sons, Ltd., circa after 1896. $45.00 – 60.00.

Tea Jar, a container with a lid, taller than a tea caddy, for storing tea leaves.

454. **Tea Jar,** 7½"h, octagonal shape, *Jappa* pattern, a version of the traditional *Willow* pattern by Gibson & Sons, circa 1912 – 1930. $250.00 – 275.00.

Teapot, a covered pot with a handle and a spout, for pouring tea. Teapots differ from coffee pots because they are shorter than coffee pots and have shorter spouts. The body of a teapot is usually wide, as compared to the vertical shape of a coffee pot.

455. **Teapot,** soft paste with a pearl ware glaze, enameled *Sprig* pattern accented with dark blue dots, unmarked, circa early 1800s. $125.00 – 150.00.

456. TEAPOT, enameled floral pattern in pink over a cream-colored glaze, unmarked, circa 1820. $450.00 – 500.00.

457. TEAPOT, Gaudy Dutch *Oyster* pattern with an Oriental style building and stylized floral designs, cobalt blue, burnt orange, and green enamels, accented with gold, unmarked, circa 1830. $450.00 – 500.00.

458. TEAPOT, Flow Blue *Chen Si* Oriental scenic pattern, J. Meir, circa 1830s. $1,400.00 – 1,600.00.

459. TEAPOT, Flow Blue *Cashmere* Oriental scenic pattern featuring a deer, unmarked, attributed to Ridgway & Morley, circa early 1840s. $1,400.00 – 1,600.00.

460. TEAPOT, Flow Blue *California* scenic pattern, unmarked except for a Registry Mark of April 2, 1849, attributed to Podmore, Walker & Co. $1,000.00 – 1,200.00.

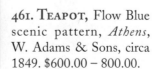

461. TEAPOT, Flow Blue scenic pattern, *Athens*, W. Adams & Sons, circa 1849. $600.00 – 800.00.

462. TEAPOT, dark gray transfer scenic pattern featuring boats, *Neptune*, unmarked, attributed to J. & G. Alcock, circa 1839 – 1846, see Williams, 1978, p. 648. $275.00 – 325.00.

463. TEAPOT, brown transfer floral pattern highlighted with red and green enamel, unmarked, circa 1840s. $225.00 – 275.00.

464. TEAPOT, *Old Japan Vase* Oriental floral pattern in burnt orange and black, unmarked, attributed to Ashworth, circa 1862. $300.00 – 350.00.

465. TEAPOT, porcelain, *Worcester Willow* pattern, Worcester, circa 1886. $300.00 – 350.00.

466. TEAPOT, traditional *Willow* pattern, Doulton, circa 1882 – 1890. $275.00 – 325.00.

467. TEAPOT, Flow Blue *Carnation* pattern, mark on base, "Royles Patent Self-Pouring, Doulton's Burslem, for J. J. Royle, Manchester, 1886." $400.00 – 500.00.

468. TEAPOT, basalt body with a black finish, Sybyl finial, a figure in the shape of a sitting draped monk, Josiah Wedgwood, circa 1892. $1,000.00 – 1,200.00.

469. TEAPOT, *Strawberry Lustre* pattern, attributed to Josiah Wedgwood, circa 1900. $400.00 – 450.00.

470. TEAPOT, Flow Blue *Quinton* floral pattern, illegible factory mark, circa early 1900s. $300.00 – 350.00.

Teapot Stand, similar to a tea tile for resting a hot teapot, except the center is raised. The tea stand is usually larger than a tea tile or a trivet. Also see Tea Tile and Tea Trivet.

471. TEA STAND, 7¾"d, octagonal shape, Mason's *Japan* pattern. Cobalt blue, a bright blue, and burnt orange are the basic colors painted on this floral pattern on a white ground. The pattern is typified by three large open blossom flowers with the center one overlaid in deep cobalt blue, G. M. & C. J. Mason, circa 1813 – 1825. $375.00 – 425.00.

Tea Strainer, a small perforated dish with a handle, for straining hot water over tea leaves.

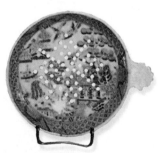

472. TEA STRAINER, 4"d, traditional *Willow* pattern, unmarked, circa early 1900s. $200.00 – 225.00.

Tea Tile, a flat piece of china, usually square or round in shape, for resting a hot teapot.

473. TEA TILE, round shape, 6"d, brown transfer of a bird returning to its nest, A. Bullock & Co., circa 1895 – 1915. $60.00 – 80.00.

474. TEA TILE, square shape, brown transfer, *Vista* scenic pattern, G. L. Ashworth, circa 1890 – 1900. $100.00 – 120.00.

475. TEA TILE, square shape, traditional *Willow* center pattern in gray and black, impressed mark, "Minton's China Works." $80.00 – 100.00.

476. TEA TILE, square shape, ornately scrolled floral and leaf pattern in a brown transfer, unmarked, circa mid- to late 1800s. $65.00 – 85.00.

477. TEA TILE, square shape, brown transfer floral pattern with hand-tinted colors, unmarked, circa mid- to late 1800s. $80.00 – 100.00.

Tea Trivet, similar to a tea tile, except a trivet has a slightly raised base or feet instead of being flat. Also see Tea Stand and Tea Tile.

478. TEA TRIVET, round shape, 5½"d, traditional *Willow* pattern, unmarked, circa late 1800s. $80.00 – 100.00.

479. TEA TRIVET, round shape, 6¼"d, Mason's *Double Landscape* Oriental scenic pattern, mauve transfer overlaid with numerous colors dominated by a dark green, G. L. Ashworth, circa 1862 – 1880. $250.00 – 300.00.

480. TEA TRIVET, brown transfer pattern with hand-tinted accents. Large flowers and leaves highlight a cameo scenic water pattern, Edge, Malkin & Co., circa 1873 – 1903. $60.00 – 80.00.

Tea Waste Bowl, a small bowl for holding the residue or "waste" from a tea cup so that the cup is clean for a fresh serving. Tea waste bowls were made as part of a tea set.

481. TEA WASTE BOWL, magenta transfer pattern, Oriental figural scene, overlaid with green, blue, and yellow enamels with gold lustre, unmarked, circa 1810. $300.00 – 350.00.

482. TEA WASTE BOWL, soft paste, enameled *Sprig* pattern of small green leaves and dots on thin pink branches, unmarked, circa early 1800s. $35.00 – 45.00.

483. TEA WASTE BOWL, traditional *Willow* pattern in Flow Blue, Doulton, circa 1891 – 1902. $150.00 – 175.00.

484. TEA WASTE BOWL, Flow Blue *Gladys* pattern, attributed to New Wharf Pottery, circa 1890 – 1894. $150.00 – 175.00.

Toast Rack, a small dish with vertical dividers for separating pieces of toast. These are more commonly found made of plated silver rather than china.

485. TOAST RACK, 4"h, small floral pattern in dark blue, unmarked, circa late 1800s. $100.00 – 125.00.

486. TOAST RACK, traditional *Willow* pattern, Grimwades, circa 1930 and after, see Godden Mark 1832. $125.00 – 150.00.

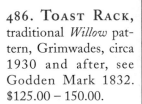

Toby Jug, a figural vessel made for either drinking or pouring ale. They are characterized by a potbellied figure, usually holding a mug of ale and wearing a tri-cornered hat. The origin of the Toby is not known, although Lewis (p. 93) notes that it may have been based on a literary figure of "Uncle Toby," or a popular song, "The Little Brown Jug," dedicated to Toby Philpot and written in 1761. Lewis also notes that the first documented Toby was dated 1785.

487. TOBY JUG, 9½"h, Whieldon type glaze, a brown mottled underglaze decoration used by Thomas Whieldon in the mid- to late 1700s, unmarked. $500.00 – 600.00.

488. TOBY JUG, 8½"h, seated figure holding a mug of ale, unmarked, circa 1880. $400.00 – 500.00.

489. TOBY JUG, 6"h, a "Merry Christmas" version decorated with holly, unmarked, circa late 1800s. $400.00 – 500.00.

490. TOBY JUGS, 5", traditional *Willow* pattern in blue on the bodies combined with hand-painted colors and black trim. Left, William Kent, circa mid-1900s; right, unmarked. $800.00 – 1,000.00 each.

Toilet Fixture, commodes and wash basins were sometimes decorated with transfer patterns.

491. TOILET FIXTURE, wash basin, with a soap shelf on each side, slate blue floral pattern, unmarked, circa late 1800s to early 1900s. $5,000.00 – 6,000.00.

492. TOILET FIXTURE, commode, slate blue floral pattern, unmarked, circa late 1800s to early 1900s. $6,000.00 – 8,000.00.

Toothbrush Holder, a vase-like open holder for toothbrushes, usually part of a matching wash set. The holders would have a hole or perforations in the base for draining purposes. A hanging rack style holder was also made. Also see Wash Set.

493. TOOTHBRUSH HOLDER, brown transfer floral and bird pattern, *Swallow,* unmarked except a Registry Mark for December 6, 1879. $70.00 – 85.00.

494. TOOTHBRUSH HOLDER, brown transfer figural pattern, unmarked, circa late 1800s. $70.00 – 85.00.

495. TOOTHBRUSH HOLDER, Art Nouveau floral style in cobalt blue, highlighted by gold lustre, Ford & Sons, circa 1890s. $100.00 – 125.00.

496. TOOTHBRUSH HOLDER, mauve transfer floral pattern with hand-tinted accents, Sampson Bridgwood & Son, circa 1890s. $60.00 – 75.00.

497. TOOTHBRUSH HOLDER, ironstone, *Moss Rose* pattern with hand-tinted accents, attributed to Whittingham, Ford & Co., circa 1868 – 1873. $60.00 – 75.00.

498. TOOTHBRUSH HOLDER, green floral transfer pattern, John Maddock, circa 1880 – 1896. $40.00 – 55.00.

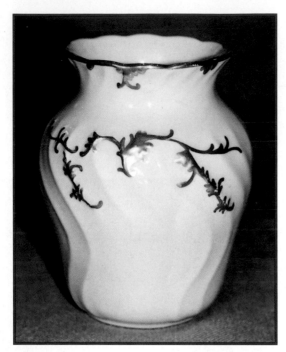

499. TOOTHBRUSH HOLDER, scrolled work on body highlighted in gold, Sampson Bridgwood & Son, circa after 1853. $50.00 – 65.00.

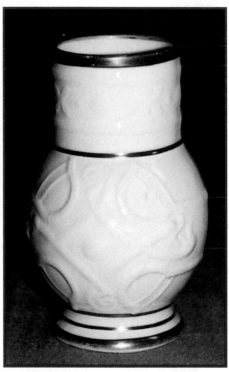

500. TOOTHBRUSH HOLDER, scrolled body designs undecorated, gold trim on rim, neck, and base, Powell, Bishop & Stonier, circa 1878 – 1891. $50.00 – 65.00.

501. TOOTHBRUSH HOLDER, Flow Blue floral pattern, *Primula*, with gold sponged accents, W. H. Grindley, Registry Mark for 1897. $60.00 – 75.00.

502. TOOTHBRUSH HOLDER, hanging rack style, Flow Blue floral pattern, *Anemone*, Bishop & Stonier, circa 1891 – 1910. $250.00 – 275.00.

Toothpick Holder, a small container for toothpicks, more commonly found in glass than china.

503. TOOTHPICK HOLDER, 2¼"h, traditional *Willow* pattern, Josiah Wedgwood, circa after 1891. $50.00 – 60.00.

Tray, a large flat ceramic dish with handles, usually rectangular in shape. Large ones were made to hold other dishes such as cups or dresser accessories. Smaller ones were used for serving various foods such as bread and celery. Also see Bread Plate.

504. TRAY, 12½"l, Alfred Meakin's *Manchu* pattern, a traditional *Willow* center pattern, circa 1930s. $150.00 – 200.00.

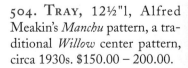

505. TRAY, 12"l, *Booths Willow* pattern, circa 1912 and after. $125.00 – 150.00.

506. TRAY, 11"l, *Variant Willow* pattern, Thomas C. Wild & Sons, Royal Albert Crown China, circa 1917 and after. $60.00 – 75.00.

507. TRAY, 17½"l, Dutch scenic pattern in blue, *Hague*, Josiah Wedgwood, circa 1876. $400.00 – 500.00.

Tumbler, a tall straight-sided drinking cup without handles, often part of a wash set. See Wash Set.

508. Tumbler, 4½"h, porcelain, slate blue floral pattern, C. T. Maling, circa late 1800s. $25.00 – 35.00.

Tureen Stand, a large platter with a raised center to hold a matching tureen.

509. Tureen Stand, brown transfer pattern, *Star,* with hand-tinted accents in red and green and a tan lustre on the rim, Hancock, Whittingham & Co., circa 1863 – 1872. $300.00 – 400.00.

510. Tureen Stand, Flow Blue Oriental floral pattern, *Ceylon,* T. Furnival & Sons, circa 1871 – 1900. $600.00 – 700.00.

Turkey Bone Dish, a wide crescent shaped dish for discarded turkey bones. Also see Bone Dish.

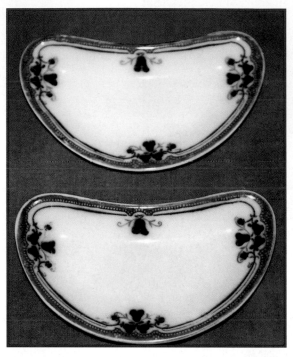

512. TURKEY BONE DISH, 6¼"l x 4"w, Flow Blue scenic pattern, *Chinese*, Josiah Wedgwood, circa 1870s. $200.00 – 225.00.

511. TURKEY BONE DISH, Flow Blue *Royston* pattern, Johnson Bros., circa early 1900s. $100.00 – 125.00. (Note the difference in the width of the regular bone dish at top and the turkey bone dish at bottom.)

Turkey Plate, a decorative plate with a turkey or turkeys as decoration made for the American market. Large platters are also found with turkey decoration.

513. TURKEY PLATE, Flow Blue transfer, Ridgways, circa early 1900s. $125.00 – 150.00.

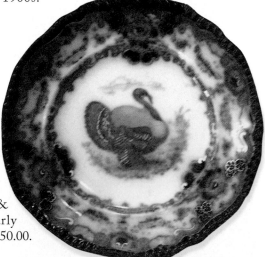

514. TURKEY PLATE, polychrome Flow Blue transfer, *Lincoln* pattern name, Bishop & Stonier, circa early 1900s. $125.00 – 150.00.

Umbrella Stand, a large open container, approximately two feet high, made to stand inside the entry of a home, to hold wet umbrellas. These are more often found made of metal rather than china.

515. UMBRELLA STAND, 23½"h, unidentified floral pattern in cobalt blue with gold sponged accents, unmarked, circa late 1800s. $500.00 – 600.00.

516. UMBRELLA STAND, 18"h, majolica, unmarked, circa late 1800s. $175.00 – 225.00.

Underplate, a platter-like dish with a recessed center to hold the base of a serving bowl, sauce boat, or sauce tureen. Also see Sauce Boat, Sauce Tureen, and Soup Tureen.

517. UNDERPLATE, brown transfer scenic pattern, *Melbourne*, Gildea & Walker, 1881 – 1885. $120.00 – 140.00.

Urn, a vase with a lid, for holding ashes of those cremated.

518. URN, 8"h, traditional *Willow* pattern, marked only with, "Made in England." $100.00 – 120.00.

Vase, a decorative open container for holding flowers, made in many different shapes and sizes, with and without handles. In my examples, the type of the shape is based on descriptions by Barber, 1914, pp. 111 – 116.

519. VASE, baluster shape, 9"h, stoneware, Art Nouveau floral and leaf décor in relief in white and cobalt blue on a rich cream colored and light olive green background with a dark brown trim on the neck and base, impressed mark, "Doulton & Slater's Patent," circa 1886 – 1914. $800.00 – 1,000.00.

520. VASE, bottle shape, 16"h, Flow Blue *Chrysanthemum* floral pattern with gold accents, George Jones, circa 1891. $400.00 – 500.00.

521. **VASE,** canteen shape, 7"h, traditional *Willow* pattern, Mintons, circa 1873. $425.00 – 475.00.

522. **VASE,** conical shape, 10"h, polychrome floral décor in a matte finish, accented with gold, Josiah Wedgwood, circa 1878 – 1900. $600.00 – 700.00.

523. **VASE,** conical shape, rich red enamel and fish scale design outlined in gold, G. L. Ashworth, circa 1920s – 1930s. $300.00 – 400.00.

524. VASE, cylinder shape, 7½"h, footed, traditional *Willow* pattern in Flow Blue, Mintons, circa 1875. $350.00 – 400.00.

525. VASE, moon or canteen shape, cobalt blue floral décor on a dark rust colored ground. The base of the vase is decorated with applied shells and seaweed, Doulton, circa early 1900s. $1,000.00 – 1,200.00.

526. VASE, oviform shape, 9"h, ring shaped handles, multicolored *Willow* pattern, Cauldon, see Godden Mark 821, circa 1905 – 1920. $450.00 – 550.00.

Vegetable Bowl, an open, oval, or round dish, eight to nine inches in diameter, without handles, for serving vegetables. Also see Serving Dish.

527. Vegetable Bowl, oval shape, 9"l, polychrome floral pattern, Mintons, circa 1891 – 1902, see Godden Mark 2713. $150.00 – 175.00.

528. Vegetable Bowl, multicolored Oriental scenic pattern, *Pekin,* also known as *Booths Variant Willow* pattern, Wood & Sons mark with pattern name, "Pekin," circa 1907 – 1910. $100.00 – 120.00.

Wash Set, a large, deep bowl and matching pitcher, designed for bathing purposes. These were usually placed on a wash stand in the bedroom. Although very utilitarian in nature, such sets were quite decorative and also included other accessories. Also see Chamber Pot, Foot Bath, Soap Dish, Sponge Dish, Toothbrush Holder, and Waste Jar.

529. Wash Set, bowl, 15"d, pitcher, 13"h, covered soap dish with liner, and razor box, Flow Blue hand-painted *Marble* pattern, unmarked, circa mid- to late 1800s. $2,500.00 – 3,000.00 set.

530. WASH SET, bowl and pitcher, Flow Blue hand-painted pattern of leaves and grapes with copper lustre, unmarked, circa mid-1800s. $3,000.00 – 4,000.00 set.

531. WASH SET, bowl and pitcher, Flow Blue Oriental scenic pattern, *Manilla*, Podmore, Walker & Co., circa 1834 – 1859. $5,000.00 – 6,000.00 set.

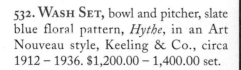

532. WASH SET, bowl and pitcher, slate blue floral pattern, *Hythe*, in an Art Nouveau style, Keeling & Co., circa 1912 – 1936. $1,200.00 – 1,400.00 set.

533. **WASH SET**, bowl, 16"d, and pitcher, 11½"h, unidentified Flow Blue floral pattern in an Art Nouveau style, unmarked, circa late 1890s. $1,800.00 – 2,000.00.

534. **WASH SET**, toothbrush holder, chamber pot, soap dish, slate blue *Napier* pattern with polychrome fruit in reserves around top borders, Keeling & Co., circa 1912 – 1936.

535. **BOWL AND PITCHER** in the *Napier* pattern. $1,800.00 – 2,000.00 complete set, which includes the wash set above.

536. WASH SET, multicolored traditional *Willow* pattern, John Tams, Ltd., Tam's Ware, circa after 1930. $1,200.00 – 1,400.00.

Waste Jar, a large covered jar with handles, a necessary accessory for wash sets.

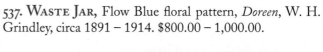

537. WASTE JAR, Flow Blue floral pattern, *Doreen,* W. H. Grindley, circa 1891 – 1914. $800.00 – 1,000.00.

538. WASTE JAR, Flow Blue floral pattern, *Syrian,* W. H. Grindley, circa 1914 – 1925. $1,000.00 – 1,200.00.

539. **WASTE JAR,** traditional *Willow* pattern in green, unmarked. $400.00 – 500.00.

Well and Tree Platter, a platter made with a deep indentation or well on one end and incised branch-like lines in the bottom. Juices or gravy from the meat on the platter would collect in the well and thus could be served easier.

540. **WELL AND TREE PLATTER,** 21"l x 17"w, footed elevation on one end, Imari colors over a blue transfer floral and scenic pattern, *Corey Hill,* unidentified manufacturer. The pattern is attributed to Ridgeways, circa 1880. $600.00 – 800.00.

541. WELL AND TREE PLATTER, 22"l, Flow Blue floral pattern, *Melsary,* accented with gold lustre, Booths, circa 1906. $500.00 – 600.00.

Wine Jug, a pitcher for wine, often decorated with a grape and vine motif.

Whey Bowl, a large, deep open bowl, for separating the curd from milk for making cheese.

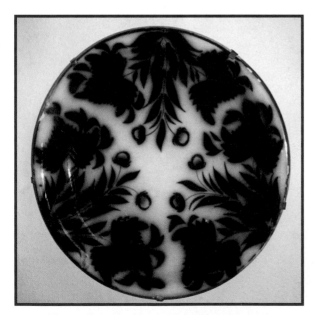

542. WHEY BOWL, 19"d, Flow Blue hand-painted pattern of leaves and small pods, unmarked, circa mid-1800s. $2,000.00 – 2,500.00.

543. WINE JUG, 7"h, white glazed earthenware, braided handle, lightly embossed body design of grapes and vines on the neck of the pitcher with the figure of a portly gentleman seated at a table with a jug and cup, marked "Spode, England," mark used by the W. T. Copeland Company after 1891. $150.00 – 175.00.

Bibliography

Bagdade, Susan and Al. *Warman's English & Continental Pottery & Porcelain.* Willow Grove, PA: Warman Publishing Co., Inc., 1987.

___. *Warman's English & Continental Pottery & Porcelain, 3rd Edition.* Iola, WI: Krause Publishing, 1998.

Barber, Edwin Atlee. *The Ceramic Collector's Glossary.* New York: Da Capo Press, 1967 (first published in New York in 1914 by the Walpole Society).

Boger, Louise-Ade. *The Dictionary of World Pottery and Porcelain.* New York: Charles Scribner's Sons, 1971.

Burton, K.J. *Pottery in England From 3500 BC – AD 1950.* South Brunswick and New York: A.S. Barnes and Company, 1975.

Caiger-Smith, Alan. *Lustre Pottery.* London: Faber and Faber, 1985.

Camehl, Ada Walker. *The Blue-China Book.* New York: Dover Publications, Inc., 1971 (originally published 1916).

Chervenka, Mark. *Guide to Fakes & Reproductions, 3rd Edition.* Iola, Wisconsin: Krause Publications, 2003.

___. "Real or Reproduction?" *Antique Trader*, February 11, 2004.

Cooper, Ronald G. *English Slipware Dishes 1650 – 1850.* New York: Transatlantic Arts, 1968.

Copeland, Robert. *Spode's Willow Pattern and Other Designs after the Chinese.* New York: Rizzoli, 1980.

Coysh, A.W. *Blue and White Transfer Ware 1780 – 1840.* Rutland, VT: A.W. Coysh, 1971.

Gaston, Mary Frank. *Blue Willow, Second Edition.* Paducah, KY: Collector Books, 1990.

___. *Collector's Encyclopedia of Art Deco.* Paducah, KY: Collector Books, 1997.

___. *Collector's Encyclopedia of English China.* Paducah, KY: Collector Books, 2002.

___. *Collector's Encyclopedia of Flow Blue China.* Paducah, KY: Collector Books, 1983.

___. *Collector's Encyclopedia of Flow Blue China, Second Series.* Paducah, KY: Collector Books, 1994.

___. *Collector's Encyclopedia of Limoges Porcelain.* Paducah, KY: Collector Books, 1980.

___ *Gaston's Blue Willow China, Third Edition.* Paducah, KY: Collector Books, 2004.

___. *Gaston's Flow Blue China, The Comprehensive Guide.* Paducah, KY: Collector Books, 2005.

Godden, Geoffrey A. *British Pottery, An Illustrated Guide.* London: Barrie & Jenkins, 1974.

___. *British Pottery and Porcelain 1780 – 1850.* New York: A.S. Barnes and Company, Inc., 1963.

___. *Encyclopedia of British Pottery and Porcelain Marks.* New York: Crown Publishers, 1964.

___. *Victorian Porcelain.* New York: Thomas Nelson & Sons, 1961.

Husfloen, Kyle (ed.). *Pottery and Porcelain Ceramic Price Guide, 2nd Edition.* Dubuque, IA: Antique Trader Books, 1997.

Huxford, Sharon and Bob (eds.). *Schroeder's Antiques Price Guide, Nineteenth Edition.* Paducah, KY: Collector Books, 2001.

Kovel, Ralph & Terry. *Kovels' New Dictionary of Marks: Pottery & Porcelain 1850 to the Present.* New York: Crown Publishers, Inc., 1986.

Lewis, Griselda. *A Collector's History of English Pottery, Fourth Revised Edition.* Woodbridge, Suffolk, England: Antique Collector's Club, Ltd., 1981; reprinted 1992 (first published in 1969 by Studio Vista Ltd.).

Little, W.L. *Staffordshire Blue.* London: B.T. Batsford, Ltd., 1969.

Mankowitz, Wolf and Reginald G. Haggar. *The Concise Encyclopedia of English Pottery and Porcelain.* New York: Hawthorne Books, Inc., n.d.

Moore, N. Hudson. *The Old China Book.* New York: Tudor Publishing Company, 1903, reprinted 1944.

Mountfield, David (comp.). *The Antique Collector's Illustrated Dictionary.* London: Hamlyn, n.d.

Rogers, Connie. *The Illustrated Encyclopedia of British Willow Ware.* Atglen, PA: Schiffer Publishing Ltd., 2004.

Schroeder Publishing Co., Inc. *Schroeder's Antiques Price Guide.* Paducah, KY: Collector Books, 2007.

Snyder, Jeffrey B. *Flow Blue, A Closer Look.* Atglen, PA: Schiffer Publishing Co. Ltd., 2000.

___. *Romantic Staffordshire Ceramics.* Atglen, PA: Schiffer Publishing Ltd., 1997.

"Victorian Staffordshire Figures." *The Collector*, p. 15, June/July 1994.

Whiter, Leonard. *Spode.* New York: Praeger Publishers, 1970.

Williams, Peter. *Wedgwood, A Collector's Guide.* Radnor, PA: Wallace-Homestead, 1992.

Williams, Petra. *Flow Blue China and Mulberry Ware.* Jeffersontown, KY: Fountain House East, 1975.

___. *Staffordshire Romantic Transfer Patterns.* Jeffersontown, KY: Fountain House East, 1978.

Zeder, Audrey B. *British Royal Commemoratives.* Lombard, IL: Wallace-Homestead, 1986.

Manufacturer Index

(BY PHOTOGRAPH NUMBER)

Pattern Index

(BY PHOTOGRAPH NUMBER)

191

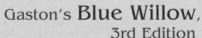
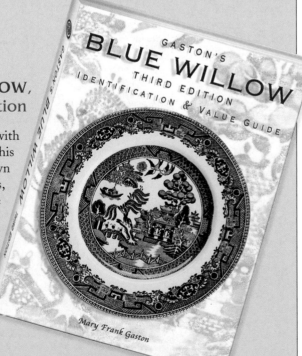